BIBLICAL SPIRITUALITY SERIES

Gospel Meditations for Lent

Coming Home to the Father

Rev. Dr. Santhiyagu Arockiyasamy, msfs

LEONINE PUBLISHERS
PHOENIX, ARIZONA

The Scripture citations used in this work are taken from the *St. Joseph New American Bible*, Giant Type edition, copyright © 1991 by Our Sunday Visitor, Huntington, IN.

Published by Leonine Publishers LLC
PO Box 8099
Phoenix, Arizona 85066
USA

ISBN-13: 978-0-9860552-5-6

Library of Congress Control Number: 2014931151

10 9 8 7 6 5 4 3 2 1

Printed in the United States of America

Visit us online at www.leoninepublishers.com
For more information: info@leoninepublishers.com

Acknowledgments

It is said that, "The smallest word of encouragement today is better than the sweetest word of compliment tomorrow." I thus remember with sincere gratitude many people who have inspired and encouraged me in many ways to complete this work.

At the outset, I would like to thank Most Rev. Earl Boyea, the bishop of the Diocese of Lansing, Michigan, for his loving support and encouragement. I also would like to express my gratitude to Rev. Dr. Abraham Vettuvelil, msfs, our Superior General; Rev. Anthony Dharma Raj, msfs, the provincial of the Southeast (India) Province of the Fransalians; and Rev. Augustine Tharappel, msfs, the vice-provincial of the USA Vice-Province, for their fraternal encouragement. I owe my gratitude to Msgr. Michael D. Hazard, V.G., Diocese of Kalamazoo, Michigan, for his guidance and Msgr. Robert D. Lunsford, Diocese of Lansing, for reading the text and giving valuable suggestions. I offer my gratitude to all my Fransalian and other priest friends for their loving support and criticism, especially to my Fransalian brother priests of the Michigan Fransalian community, as they walked with me and showed their love, concern, and support in completing this work. I must express my sincere gratitude and appreciation to the Diocesan Publications in Lansing for the permission to use some of the Lenten clip art pictures, to Mr. Tom Valli, J.D., for his timely help in proofreading the text, and to Mrs. Sylvia Kaake for the permission to use the painting of Jesus from her grandmother's kitchen, and all my friends, especially the staff and parishioners of St. Mary parish in Flint, Michigan, for their motivation and encouragement, which inspired me to write this book.

I hope that this book will inspire and motivate you during this holy season to find Jesus in your life and experience His love.

In love and gratitude,

Rev. Dr. Santhiyagu Arockiyasamy, msfs

Dedication

To my Fransalian Missionaries
Who in their dedication and missionary commitment
Sacrificed their life to proclaim the Gospel of Jesus Christ
And planted the seed of faith at home and in overseas missions

Contents

Foreword

The annual observance of the season of Lent calls each of us to a deeper conversion with its twofold dimension of repentance and growth in our baptismal graces. We seek to grow in love of God and one another through prayer, fasting, and almsgiving.

In this book, Fr. Santhiyagu Arockiyasamy, msfs, offers us the fruit of his spiritual reflections on the Lenten readings. His meditations are complemented by passages from the writings of the great spiritual director of souls, St. Francis de Sales. Salesian spirituality is noted for assisting us to translate spiritual principles to our ordinary lives in practical ways.

These meditations foster a desire for holiness and offer common-sense ways to grow spiritually through prayer, reception of the sacraments, and in our relations with one another. Occasional stories illustrate a point, and questions in each meditation assist us in applying the fruits of our prayers.

My prayer and hope is that those who use this book—ordinary people in ordinary circumstances—will be led more deeply into the Paschal Mystery, imitating Jesus and growing in love of God and one another.

✠ Earl Boyea
  Bishop of Lansing, Michigan
  January 15, 2014

Introduction

The Sage in the book of Proverbs writes, "Happy the man who finds wisdom, the man who gains understanding! For her profit is better than profit in silver, and better than gold is her revenue; Long life is in her right hand, in her left are riches and honor; Her ways are pleasant ways, and all her paths are peace" (Prov 3: 13-14, 16-17). This little book comes wrapped with seeds of wisdom from the Gospel message of Jesus and the spiritual wisdom of St. Francis de Sales. Its purpose is to inspire, encourage, motivate, and enlighten readers in their Lenten journey to understand the true meaning of Jesus' Passion, death, and resurrection and to find Jesus in their lives.

Once a believer shared his faith experience as follows: "I was a neurotic for years, suffering its consequences. I was anxious, depressed, and selfish. Everyone was advising me constantly to change. I resented them, but I agreed with them, and I wanted to change. I tried my best but simply couldn't change even a little bit, no matter how hard I tried. What hurt me the most was that like others even my best friend kept insisting that I must change. So I got frustrated; felt powerless and trapped. Then, one day, my friend said to me, 'Don't change. I love you just as you are.' Those words were music to my ears: 'Don't change. Don't change. Don't change….I love you as you are.' Listening to those words, I relaxed. I came out alive. And suddenly I changed. Now I know that I couldn't really change until I found someone who would love me whether I changed or not. Then, I prayed, 'Is this how you love me, O God?'" (Anthony de Mello, *The Song of the Bird*, 67-68).

Yes, indeed. God the Father loves us in Jesus not because we are good and lovable but that we would become good and lovable. The season of Lent brings us the good news that God is anxiously waiting like a prodigal Father for our homecoming to experience His love and forgiveness. Are you ready to return to the Father in repentance? If you realize that Jesus asks you to spend just five to ten minutes of your time for Him in the morning, or in the evening, or during the day as you choose, surely this book can be of good help for you to listen to God's word, reflect quietly, and pray confidently during this Lent.

Rev. Dr. Santhiyagu Arockiyasamy, msfs
St. Mary Church, 2500 N Franklin Ave, Flint, MI 48506

Our Lenten Journey

Returning to the Father

"Even now, says the Lord, return to me
With your whole heart, with fasting, and
Weeping, and mourning; rend your hearts,
Not your garments" (Joel 2: 12-13).

Ash Wednesday

Joel 2: 12-18; 2Cor 5: 20-6: 2; Mt 6: 1-6, 16-18

Preparation: Take a few minutes of silence, setting aside all your worries and anxieties, and become aware of the divine presence.

Listening to God's Word: When you fast, do not look gloomy like the hypocrites. They neglect their appearance, so that they may appear to others to be fasting. Amen, I say to you, they have received their reward. But when you fast, anoint your head and wash your face, so that you may not appear to be fasting, except to your Father who is hidden. And your Father who sees what is hidden will repay you (Mt 6: 16-18).

The Time is Now

The Liturgy of the Word at the beginning of the season of Lent invites us to look back into our life with repentance for renewal in life. Repentance is the inner attitude of the heart with a sense of remorse for the sins committed against God and others. It is an awareness of our sinfulness and readiness to renew ourselves with determination for greater growth. St. Paul teaches, "Put away the old self of your former life and be renewed in the Spirit; and put on the new self created according to the likeness of God in holiness" (Eph 4: 22-24). Our efforts to avoid sin and live a renewed life will be the concrete expression of our sincere repentance. Once a first-century Rabbi told his followers, "Repent one day before your death." He often repeated this slogan to the disciples. One day they asked him, "But how does anyone know? One might die any day; it could be tomorrow, next week, next month or next year." The Rabbi said, "Then, repent one day before your death." The message is repent "NOW" and be renewed "TODAY." God says through Prophet Joel, "Even now return to me with your whole heart. Rend your hearts, not your garments" (Joel 2: 12a, 13a). Since God is kind and merciful, ready to forgive, He invites us to come to Him with repentance of heart without delay (cf. v. 13b). As St. Paul says, "Now is a very acceptable time; behold, now is the day of salvation" (cf. 2Cor 6: 2b). The need for a renewed life in repentance cannot be postponed for a convenient time.

Our renewal should begin "NOW," and the change in our approach and attitudes toward life and people must take place "NOW."

Lent as the season of grace is the opportune time to be reconciled with God and with one another. This invitation to repentance and renewal is not a threat of punishment but an invitation to new life, as God in His compassionate love does not want us to be punished but saved. The actions of fasting, weeping, and mourning express the seriousness of our sins and the need for sincere repentance. Hence, Jesus teaches us in the Gospel today, "When you fast, do not look gloomy like the hypocrites. They neglect their appearance, so that they may appear to others to be fasting. But when you fast, anoint your head and wash your face, so that you may not appear to be fasting, except to your Father who is in heaven" (Mt 6: 16-18a). Our acts of penance should not be for the sake of an outward show of our piety. Rather, they must be the concrete expression of true love from the heart with the attitude of determination to repent, reconcile, and renew ourselves TODAY. During this Lenten season, let us acknowledge our sinfulness and failures, and come back to the Lord as the prodigal son, saying, "I shall get up and go to my Father" (Lk 15: 18). God our Father is affectionately waiting for our return, saying, "Even now come back to me and get reconciled. Now is the day of salvation." How do I understand the need for my renewal now in the present? What change should this Lenten season bring in my life?

Wisdom from St. Francis de Sales: There are three things regarding fasting. First, your fast should be entire and universal; that is, you should make all the members of your body and the powers of your soul fast. Second, do not observe your fast or perform your good works for the eyes of the others. Third, you do all your actions and consequently your fasting to please God alone" (cf. Nuns of the Visitation (trans.), *The Sermons of St. Francis de Sales for Lent*, 2, 11-12).

Prayer: Let us pray with the Psalmist: Lord, I know my offenses; my sin is always before me. I have sinned against you. Have mercy on me, O God in your goodness, in your compassion blot out my offenses, in your mercy wash away all my guilt and cleanse me from sins (Ps. 51: 1-6).

Thursday after Ash Wednesday

Deut 30: 15-20; Lk 9: 22-25

Preparation: Take a few minutes of silence, setting aside all your worries and anxieties, and become aware of the divine presence.

Listening to God's Word: He said, "The Son of Man must suffer greatly and be rejected by the elders, the chief priests, and the scribes, and be killed and on the third day be raised." Then he said to all, "If anyone wishes to come after me, he must deny himself and take up his cross daily and follow me. For whoever wishes to save his life will lose it, but whoever loses his life for my sake will save it" (Lk 9: 22-24).

Choosing the Cross to Choose Life

As believers in Jesus, the purpose of our life is to choose life and not destruction, and so the season of Lent echoes the need for repentance and renewal in life. In light of this clarion call, the liturgy of today brings us the teachings of Jesus about choosing life by choosing the way of the Cross. He says, "If anyone wishes to come after me, he must deny himself and take up his cross daily and follow me" (Lk 9: 23). In our Christian circle when we speak of the cross today, we refer to anything and anyone causing suffering, pain, problems, and hardships. In the days of Jesus, anyone who spoke about the cross was literally referring to the wooden cross used by the Romans for carrying out the excruciating public execution of those convicted of crimes and revolt against the rulers. In the teaching of Jesus, cross refers to the challenges and trials, including death, as a consequence of the choice made in following the Lord's way of life. In this background, "taking up the cross daily" expresses the nature of our faith life that includes difficulties, struggles, and suffering in making choices for God. "Following Jesus" implies the spirit of determination and perseverance to walk with Him despite our human shortcomings and failures. "Taking up the cross" implies readiness to face challenges in life without giving up. In this light, to follow the way of Jesus by courageously facing the trials in daily life is to choose life in its fullness. So Jesus assures us, "For whoever wishes to save his life will lose it, but whoever loses his life for my sake will save it" (v. 24). The call of this holy season to repentance and renewal is a call to be faithful in following the way of Jesus without compromise.

Jesus faithfully fulfilled God's plan of human salvation by reaching out to those on the margins, extending them God's forgiveness, sharing meals with them in fraternal love, and even violating the formal religious traditions when bringing life to others. This eventually brought opposition from the religious and political leaders. He knew that this would lead to His suffering and death, yet He remained loyal in fulfilling the Father's plan for the world without compromise and chose the way of the Cross to bring life to humanity. As believers, if we follow Jesus to choose the way of the Cross within our own living situations, we will choose life at its best, understanding its true value and meaning. God said to the people of Israel, "I have set before you life and death, the blessing and the curse. Choose life, then, that you and your descendants may live" (Deut 30: 19). "The proof of love is in the works. Where love exists, it works great things. But when it ceases to act, it ceases to exist" (Pope St. Gregory the Great). Indeed, we choose life by loving God and others as Jesus has taught us. We choose death by refusing to love. What is my attitude in facing the challenges and trials in my faith life? What is my choice—to choose fullness of life through Jesus or losing life by deliberately refusing to love?

Wisdom from St. Francis de Sales: The true Christian, or to use the term appropriate for you, the true religious, who is tending toward Christian perfection, should, contrary to all the reasoning of human prudence, place all his (her) perfection in the folly of the Cross, because it was in this folly of the Cross that our Lord was made perfect. So all the saints have endeavored to become wise in this folly and, for this, suffered all the contempt, censures, and humiliations which came to them from the worldly wise. Perfection of the Cross requires that we endure labors, persecutions, and reprehensions for justice' sake. This wisdom is wholly contrary to that of the world (Visitation, *The Sermons of SFS for Lent,* 166).

Prayer: Dear Jesus, thank you for teaching me the meaning of the Cross in my life. Help me to face the challenges and trials in life with optimism to follow you in steadfastness.

Friday after Ash Wednesday

Is 58: 1-9a; Mt 9: 14-15

Preparation: Take a few minutes of silence, setting aside all your worries and anxieties, and become aware of the divine presence.

Listening to God's Word: Then the disciples of John approached him and said, "Why do we and the Pharisees fast much but your disciples do not fast?" Jesus answered them, "Can the wedding guests mourn as long as the bridegroom is with them? The days will come when the bridegroom is taken away from them, and then they will fast" (Mt 9: 14-15).

Personal Acts of Piety

Spiritual devotions such as prayer, fasting, abstinence, and almsgiving practiced at the wrong time, the wrong place, and with false intentions would be ineffective at best and even sinful. As we enter the season of Lent, people naturally practice certain acts of piety to express their Lenten devotions. So, we hear from people who speak about their Lenten devotional practices like spending some extra time in prayer, or saying extra prayers, taking up fasting, even for all forty days, abstaining from certain food such as sweets, candy, chocolate, etc. We would find all such actions easy and convenient. But the Liturgy of the Word today invites us to understand that God demands something more than all these: namely, a change in our behaviors and attitudes. The disciples of John the Baptist and the Pharisees tried to fulfill God's will by leading an austere life of penance like the Dead Sea scribes. They made special efforts to impose upon themselves penance beyond what was generally expected, whereas they found Jesus and his disciples not undertaking rigorous fasts. So they asked Jesus, "Why do your disciples not fast?" (Mt 9: 14). The question concerns an individual's private fast as a devotional practice. In response to them, Jesus explained about the proper time of fasting. As Jesus during his ministry revealed the nearness of God's reign, it was an inappropriate time for rigorous fasting or mourning but for rejoicing and celebration (cf. Mt 4: 17).

As long as Jesus the bridegroom was with the disciples, there was no need for fasting or mourning (cf. Mt 9: 15). But after the death and resurrection of Jesus it was the appropriate time for the Christians to fast and do penance as part of their devotions. However, our devotional practices such as prayer, fasting, and doing sacrifices must lead us closer to God and not merely to fulfill rituals or our personal interests. Therefore, Isaiah says, "On your fast day you carry out your own pursuits, and drive all your laborers. Yes, your fast ends in quarrelling and fighting, striking with wicked claw" (Is 58: 3b-4). Such attitudes and actions are not the sign of true repentance and this is not the kind of fasting that God desires. The prophet is addressing here the issue of sincerity and integrity in our spiritual practices. God is only pleased with our devotions that are accompanied by acts of mercy and love for defending the cause of the poor, caring for the needy, providing justice, feeding the hungry, clothing the naked, sheltering the homeless, and encouraging the discouraged (cf. Is 58: 6-7). In this light, how meaningful are my devotional practices during this Lent and how do they affect my personal life? Do my acts of piety fulfill Jesus' program of mercy toward others, or instead carry out my own personal interests?

Wisdom from St. Francis de Sales: O God, how spiritually beneficial and profitable is a consideration of your Cross and Passion! Can we contemplate our Savior's humility on the Cross without becoming humble and having some affection for humiliation? Can we see His obedience without being obedient? Certainly not! No one has ever looked upon our Lord crucified and remained dead or sick. On the other hand, all who have died have done so because they were unwilling to gaze upon Him, just as Israelites died who were unwilling to gaze upon the serpent that Moses had raised upon the pole (Visitation, *The Sermons of SFS for Lent*, 181-182).

Prayer: Dear Jesus, thank you for revealing the presence of God's reign as a time of rejoicing. Help me to carry out my devotional practices in true faith and love for you and my neighbor.

Saturday after Ash Wednesday

Is 58: 9b-14; Lk 5: 27-32

Preparation: Take a few minutes of silence, setting aside all your worries and anxieties, and become aware of the divine presence.

Listening to God's Word: Then Levi gave a great banquet for him in his house, and a large crowd of tax collectors and others were at table with them. The Pharisees and their scribes complained to his disciples, saying, "Why do you eat and drink with tax collectors and sinners?" Jesus said to them in reply, "Those who are healthy do not need a physician, but the sick do. I have not come to call the righteous to repentance but sinners" (Lk 5: 29-32).

The Power of Fraternal Fellowship

In the ancient world, "table-fellowship" symbolized spiritual unity. When Jesus proclaimed the dawn of God's reign with the fulfillment of the Messianic age (Mt 4: 17), the thrust of His message was "to save the sinners." While the social system of the time disregarded certain groups of people, labeling them as unclean, outcast, and sinners and ill-treated them in terms of discrimination and segregation, Jesus wholeheartedly welcomed them and engaged them in banqueting-fellowship (cf. Lk 5: 29-30). What did the inclusion of public sinners and the marginalized in Jesus' fellowship reveal about God's reign which Jesus proclaimed? This is the issue reflected in today's Gospel narrative. Jesus in His response used the medical imagery of a physician who restores health to those who are sick (Lk 5: 31). Like the physician, Jesus the Messiah came to heal and save those who were regarded as sinners and outcast in the society. Therefore, He said, "I have not come to call the righteous to repentance but sinners" (Lk 5: 32). Here, repentance is metanoia which involves change of life, renewal at the personal and social level, a new beginning, and a new orientation in one's life. Through His table-fellowship with the so-called sinners, Jesus offered them the opportunity to experience God's love and compassion where they felt welcomed and honored and experienced personal healing and acceptance.

Thus, Jesus' fellowship is not one in which the righteous are separated from the sinners, but it is a community of accessibility and availability where human persons are welcomed and loved, valued, and cared for. In such a community of fellowship, relationships are renewed and life has a new beginning. The wholehearted response of Levi to Jesus' call indicates his interior change of heart and his total commitment to follow Jesus. The Good News of Jesus' identification with our sinful humanity requires a new beginning and reorientation in our life as a spiritual journey of metanoia. God said through the prophet Isaiah, "If you remove from your midst oppression, false accusation and malicious speech; if you bestow your bread on the hungry and satisfy the afflicted; then light shall rise for you in the darkness" (Is 58: 9b-10). Lent is a joyful season which offers us the wonderful opportunity to mend our broken relationships with God and others. Let us learn to create in our communities a sense of fraternal fellowship in loving solidarity and offer people the opportunity to experience God's loving welcome and acceptance. How do I understand the meaning of "table-fellowship" in my life? What do I do in my families and communities to create opportunities for others to experience God's grace of cordial welcome and to foster a new beginning?

Wisdom from St. Francis de Sales: It is at the foot of this Cross that we should remain always. It is the place where the imitators of our sovereign Master and Savior ordinarily abide. For it is from the Cross that they receive the heavenly liqueur of holy charity. It streams out in great profusion from a divine source, the bosom of our good God's divine mercy. He loved us with a love so firm, so solid, so ardent and so persevering that death itself could not cool it in the least. Such ought to be our love for the neighbor: firm, ardent, solid and persevering (Visitation, *The Sermons of SFS for Lent*, 97).

Prayer: Dear Jesus, your table-fellowship symbolizes your banquet of salvation. Guide me to foster the spirit of fraternal unity and brotherhood to overcome division among us.

First Week

Our Struggle – Our Temptation

Monday of the First Week of Lent

Lev 19: 1-2, 11-18; Mt 25: 31-46

Preparation: Take a few minutes of silence, setting aside all your worries and anxieties, and become aware of the divine presence.

Listening to God's Word: Then the king will say to those on his right, "Come, you who are blessed by my Father. Inherit the kingdom prepared for you from the foundation of the world. For I was hungry and you gave me food, I was thirsty and you gave me drink, a stranger and you welcomed me, naked and you clothed me, ill and you cared for me, in prison and you visited me" (Mt 25: 34-36).

Loving God in Others

We know from our experience that hatred and rejection cause turmoil and meaninglessness, but kindness begets kindness. Even a little act of kindness builds us up, strengthens our spirit, and opens up a new world of people around us. That is why people, touched by acts of kindness and love, remember them forever in their life. Jesus began his public ministry with the proclamation of the nearness of God's reign: "The time is fulfilled. The kingdom of God is at hand. Repent and believe in the Good News" (Mk 1: 15). At the final judgment, people will be judged and rewarded based on their response to this divine call and the Good News preached by Jesus. The Gospel narrative about the final judgment urges us to find God in others, especially the poor, the suffering, and the marginalized. We are to love God by loving and caring for others. Jesus enacted his proclamation about God's reign by performing acts of compassion and kindness to those who were afflicted, neglected, and suffering. When He generously forgave sinners and shared fellowship with everyone, the people indeed experienced the nearness of a loving God.

As followers of Jesus, we are impelled to prove our love for God by our acts of kindness and love toward those who are wounded, discouraged, sick, and suffering. You and I may be the ones who can make the difference in the lives of such people by finding and loving Jesus in them.

This is the essence of our Christian faith because God takes seriously our human actions. So Jesus affirmed, "Amen, I say to you, whatever you did for one of these least brothers of mine, you did for me" (Mt 25: 40), and "whatever you did not do for one of these least ones, you did not do for me" (v. 45). This is the nature of the kingdom-oriented spirituality of Jesus which is people centered. When we find Jesus in others and respond to their need with human compassion, or fail to respond, we are in fact responding to Jesus himself. The author of Leviticus (19: 1-2, 11-18) explains that God directed the people not to do those things that are destructive and harmful to others. As a people chosen to be holy, Israel had to be compassionate as God is holy and compassionate toward them. Lent is the right time to deepen our understanding that God's compassionate love provokes us to be a people of compassion. Do I make efforts to seek God in others by my acts of compassion and kindness? What does it mean for me to be compassionate in my life as God is compassionate to me?

Wisdom from St. Francis de Sales: Love has its source in the heart, and we cannot love our neighbor too much or go to excess, provided love continues to reside in the heart. However, our external demonstration of love may err or get out of control, passing the limits and rules of reason. The glorious Saint Bernard says that the limit of loving God is loving God without limits; His love must spread its root as widely as possible. And what is said about love of God must also apply to love of our neighbor, so long as the love of God is greater and holds first place in our hearts (St. Francis De Sales, *Spiritual Treatises IV*, from *Every Day with Saint Francis de Sales*, 22).

Prayer: Dear Jesus, thank you for revealing the nature of God's kingdom as people centered. Help me to seek God in others by truly loving them so that I may experience God's compassion.

Tuesday of the First Week of Lent

Is 55: 10-11; Mt 6: 7-15

Preparation: Take a few minutes of silence, setting aside all your worries and anxieties, and become aware of the divine presence.

Listening to God's Word: In praying, do not babble like the pagans, who think that they will be heard because of their many words. Do not be like them. This is how you are to pray: Our Father in heaven, hallowed be your name, your kingdom come, your will be done on earth as in heaven. Your Father knows what you need before you ask him. If you forgive others their transgressions, your heavenly Father will forgive you (Mt 6: 7-10, 14).

The Abba Prayer

Prayer forms the heart of every religion's traditions and teachings. Without prayer, devotional practices have no meaning. We find in the Gospel accounts that Jesus had not imposed strict rules on the disciples about how they should pray and how often they should pray. The only prayer Jesus taught the disciples was the "Our Father." It summarizes succinctly the heart of Jesus' spirituality which is both oriented toward the realization of God's kingdom and that it is people centered. So this prayer takes the center place in the prayer life of the Church and of the people. Like the other Jewish Rabbis and John the Baptist had taught their disciples, Jesus too taught His disciples about the nature of prayer and proper attitude when praying. As we heard in today's Gospel, Jesus, in teaching us how to pray, emphasizes certain essential elements to characterize our prayer: there must be no showiness or fabling with many words and terminologies, no special opportunities or circumstances are needed, and no auspicious time or sacred rubrics are important either. Our prayer must be communitarian and it must come from the heart. We must have the proper attitudes of deep trust, total surrender, and child-like confidence in God.

We should enter into prayer with the realization of the Father-child relationship between God and us. We need to have the awareness of God's holiness and kindness and of our own lowliness and human weaknesses. Jesus teaches us that while praying the Our Father, we must learn to practice in life what we ask from God, because what we do to others will be the measure of what we will receive from God. So Jesus says, "If you forgive, you will be forgiven" (Mt 6: 14). St. Paul too teaches us "to be kind to one another, tender hearted and to forgive one another as God has forgiven us in Christ" (Eph 4: 32). God's Word spoken in love does not return in vain but fulfills God's purpose (cf. Is 55: 11). Whenever we come in prayer calling God our Father, we must be ready to do the Father's will and not our own will. "Prayer is not asking. It is a longing of the soul. It is daily admission of one's weakness. It is better in prayer to have a heart without words than words without a heart" (Mahatma Gandhi). How do I understand the meaning of the Lord's Prayer in the context of my own life situations? Do I place my trust and confidence in God, experiencing God's dearness and nearness while praying?

Wisdom from St. Francis de Sales: In prayer we approach God and place ourselves in his presence for two reasons: first, it is to render to God the honor and praise we owe him, and this can be done without his speaking to us or our speaking to him. We can fulfill this duty by acknowledging that he is our God and we are his creatures (Ps 95: 6-7), and by remaining before him. We do this simply to demonstrate and prove our willingness and gratitude to be in his service which is a mark of great perfection. Second, it is to speak to him and to hear him speak to us through inspiration and the inner stirrings of our heart (Peronne M. Thibert (trans.), SFS, Jane de Chantal, *Letters of Spiritual Direction,* 100-101).

Prayer: Dear Jesus, thank you for revealing God as a loving and compassionate Father. Guide me to approach Him with a child-like confidence, and never to doubt or distrust His love.

Wednesday of the First Week of Lent

Jonah 3: 1-10; Lk 11: 29-32

Preparation: Take a few minutes of silence, setting aside all your worries and anxieties, and become aware of the divine presence.

Listening to God's Word: While still more people gathered in the crowd, he said to them, "This generation is an evil generation; it seeks a sign, but no sign will be given it, except the sign of Jonah. Just as Jonah became a sign to the Ninevites, so will the Son of Man be to this generation" (Lk 11: 29-30).

Responding to the Signs

In our daily life, there are many signs that we faithfully follow for keeping the law and maintaining order, protecting others and ourselves from dangers, etc. In today's Gospel narrative, Jesus invites us to respond to the signs of our times for receiving God's blessings for positive growth. When God called Jonah, he behaved like a reluctant and comical parody of a prophet. His call to be a prophet was not merely to bring about the conversion of the Ninevites. It was a story of his conversion too. At the first encounter, he tried to escape from God by refusing to go to Nineveh (cf. Jonah 1: 2-3). But the great storm in the sea was the sign for him to accept the divine call to preach God's word to the people of Nineveh (vv. 4, 11-17). Moreover, the preaching of Jonah was a sign for the people to turn away from their evil ways and believe in God (cf. Jonah 3: 3-15). Their sincere repentance was the sign for God to change his plan of punishment. Therefore, "When God saw what they did, how they turned away from evil ways, God changed his mind about the calamity that he would bring upon them and he did not do it" (v. 10). We notice here how everyone responded to the signs given them: Jonah responded in faith to the sign of his prophetic call, the Ninevites responded in conversion to the sign of the prophet's preaching, and God responded to the sign of the people's repentance. Such a faith-filled response to the signs of the time resulted in a positive outcome.

When Jesus is compared with the prophet Jonah, He (along with His preaching and life-giving actions of compassion) becomes the sign of God's saving presence among us (cf. Lk 11: 31-32). Jesus reveals how God is committed to loving us, forgiving us, and saving us from sin and death. God's love revealed through Jesus is a sign for us to return to the Father in repentance and renewal. Whenever we come to God in prayer, through the reading of the Scripture, or in the celebration of the sacraments, particularly the sacraments of Reconciliation and the Eucharist, it is a sign of God's compassionate love for us. He calls us persistently to rely on Him alone. The signs of our world such as positive developments, prosperity, and human achievements constantly remind us to gratefully appreciate the marvelous goodness and blessings of God. Even adverse events and experiences, namely family problems, marriage issues, social problems, and personal experiences of crisis are meaningful signs that help us to see God's presence and to listen to Jesus' voice during challenging moments. These signs should not lead us to doubt the power of Jesus in our life but can teach us to approach life with optimism and faith. How do I respond to the signs of my life—positively or negatively? Do I see the adverse events in my life as signs that teach me to rely on Jesus and walk with Him in faith?

Wisdom from St. Francis de Sales: You must hate your faults, but you should do so calmly and peacefully, without fuss or anxiety. You must be patient when you see them and benefit from seeing your own lowliness. Unless you do this, your imperfections, of which you are acutely conscious, will disturb you even more and thus grow stronger, for nothing is more favorable to the growth of these weeds than our anxiety and over-eagerness to get rid of them (Thibert, *Letters of Spiritual Direction,* 161).

Prayer: Dear Jesus, your words and actions are signs of your call to repentance and renewal. Guide me during this Lent to listen to your voice and come back to you in repentance.

Thursday of the First Week of Lent

Esther C: 12, 14-16, 23-25; Mt 7: 7-12

Preparation: Take a few minutes of silence, setting aside all your worries and anxieties, and become aware of the divine presence.

Listening to God's Word: Ask and it will be given to you; seek and you will find; knock and the door will be opened to you. For everyone who asks, receives; and the one who seeks, finds; and to the one who knocks, the door will be opened (Mt 7: 7-8).

Perseverance in Prayer

When children want something from their parents, they keep on asking until they get what they want. They are confident that their parents will yield to their request. In the context of teaching the disciples about their inner disposition needed for effective prayer, Jesus instructed them "to ask, seek, and knock." What does this mean? What should I ask for? What should I seek? Whose door must I knock at? Once a father and his five year old son were working in their garden. The father told the little boy to remove a big stone that was lying on the path way. The boy tried to move it but could not budge it even an inch. So he said, "Dad, I am not able to move it." "Use all your strength and effort, and you can do it," the father insisted. The little boy tried all the more harder but could not move the stone. So he again said to his father, "Dad, I tried with all my effort and did my best. I could not do it." The boy began to cry because of his inability and helplessness. The father approached the little boy and said, "Son, if you are not able to move the stone with your own effort, you should have asked me for help. Why didn't you call me?" This is what prayer is: seeking God and crying out for his help in everything. In today's Gospel, Jesus teaches us, "Ask and it will be given to you; seek and you will find; knock and the door will be opened to you" (Mt 7: 7). The three terms "ask, seek, and knock" are active verbs which imply continuous actions and initiative on the part of those involved in such actions. So, Jesus says, "For everyone who asks, receives; and the one who seeks, finds; and to the one who knocks, the door will be opened" (v. 8).

It is not that God as our loving Father does not know our needs. He knows everything about us and shows extreme concern and care for us. Yet, since it is we who are in need, we must own the responsibility and take the initiative to call out to God for His help with a child-like attitude. Moreover, when we ask for something, we trust that it will be given. When we seek for something, we are hopeful that we will find it. When we knock at the doors of our dear ones or neighbors, we are confident that they will open the door to respond to our needs. Without the attitudes of trust, hope, and confidence, the actions of asking, seeking, and knocking will be meaningless and fruitless. When we come before God in prayer, we must have the positive attitudes of trust, hope, and confidence that God will listen to us and answer our prayers. Consider Esther who approached God for help with an attitude of trust and confidence in God's power to save her people (cf. Esther C: 23-25). We know from our experience that we don't receive from God everything we ask for. Yet, we should not give up our efforts when God does not answer us according to our expectations. Our heavenly Father who is kind and compassionate will provide our needs generously though he might delay to provide our particular needs as we expect. Therefore, we must persevere in our efforts of asking and seeking God's grace and knocking at God's door for help. Then, our prayer will become efficacious in due time as God wills it. Do I expect God to act according to my wishes and desires, or do I act according to God's plan for me? In praying, do I persevere in asking, seeking, and knocking for God's help, or do I give up because I don't get my desired results?

Wisdom from St. Francis de Sales: Trees bear fruit only because of the presence of the sun, some sooner, and some later, some every year, and others every three years, not all of them always yielding equal harvests. We are very fortunate to be able to remain in the presence of God; so let us be content that he will make us bear our fruit sooner or later, every day or only occasionally, according to his good pleasure to which we should be fully resigned (Thibert, *Letters of Spiritual Direction,* 109).

Prayer: Dear Jesus, thank you for teaching me to pray, trusting in the Father's goodness. Help me to pray with perseverance, surrendering to do, not my will, but the Father's will in my life.

20 BIBLICAL SPIRITUALITY SERIES

Friday of the First Week of Lent

Ez 18: 21-28; Mt 5: 20-26

Preparation: Take a few minutes of silence, setting aside all your worries and anxieties, and become aware of the divine presence.

Listening to God's Word: But I say to you, whoever is angry with his brother will be liable to judgment. Therefore, if you bring your gift to the altar, and there recall that your brother has anything against you, leave your gift there at the altar, go first and be reconciled with your brother, and then come and offer your gift (Mt 5: 22a, 23-24).

Defusing Anger

From our daily life experiences we know that more problems are caused in the family and society by people's anger and resentment against each other. As long as we keep our anger alive against ourselves or others, it will nurture enmity and hatred. It will grow causing acts of violence and even murder to happen. As we heard in the Gospel today, Jesus warns us against the dire consequences of anger if we foster it to grow. He says, "You have heard that it was said to your ancestors, 'You shall not kill; and whoever kills will be liable to judgment.' But I say to you, whoever is angry with his brother, will be liable to judgment" (Mt 5: 21). Here Jesus emphasizes that anger as the root cause of evils is as serious a sin as the act of murder itself. Usually getting provoked to murder is a very rare temptation, but getting stirred up in anger is a common experience that could lead to vengeance and hatred, culminating in unjustified acts of violence. Therefore, it is not enough for believers to restrain from external actions that are sinful and harmful. They also should find out the root cause for their evil actions, such as anger, and overcome it.

Long before we let our ruptured relationships with others reach the disastrous stage of causing alienation and hostility, we must work out ways to defuse our anger and reach reconciliation. Without an inner change of attitudes to defuse anger, even our worship and liturgical sacrifices become meaningless and unacceptable. For this reason, Jesus advocates reconciliation with others before coming into God's presence for prayer and worship (v. 24). As we hear from the prophet Ezekiel, God's way is the way of mercy and forgiveness. God assures us that if wicked persons follow the commandments, turn away from all their sins and evil ways, and do what is right and righteous, they shall live (cf. Ez 18: 21). Therefore, Jesus advocates three ways to defuse anger and break the spiral of evil actions. First, we must avoid insulting and demeaning one another by words or actions. Second, our liturgical sacrifices cannot cover up our broken and strained relationships. Honest reconciliation is the only way. Third, we should not allow division and conflict to escalate to the point of litigation and revenge-taking. Let us know that anybody can become angry—that is easy, but to be angry with the right person, to the right degree, at the right time, for the right purpose, and in the right way—that is not within everybody's power and is not easy to do (Aristotle). How do I face the situation in which I am provoked to anger? Do I make efforts to defuse anger and get reconciled, or do I keep fostering anger and hatred against others?

Wisdom from St. Francis de Sales: This miserable life is only a progressive journey to the happy life to come. Therefore let us not be angry at all with one another on the way. Let us walk in the company of our brothers and sisters gently, peacefully and kindly. Further, I tell you very plainly and without any exception: do not become angry at all if that is possible. Do not accept any pretext whatever to open the door of your heart to anger (SFS, *Introduction to the Devout Life (IDL), Part III*, Ch. 8, p. 189).

Prayer: Dear Jesus, thank you for motivating me to be loving and considerate toward others. Inspire me to defuse my anger and cultivate the virtue of patience and forgiveness.

Saturday of the First Week of Lent

Deut 26: 16-19; Mt 5: 43-48

Preparation: Take a few minutes of silence, setting aside all your worries and anxieties, and become aware of the divine presence.

Listening to God's Word: But I say to you, love your enemies, and pray for those who persecute you, that you may be children of your heavenly Father, for he makes his sun rise on the bad and the good, and causes rain to fall on the just and the unjust. So be perfect, just as your heavenly Father is perfect (Mt 5: 44-45, 48).

The Divine Technique

For most of us, loving and forgiving those (our enemies) who harm and wound us is the most difficult thing to do in life. Once on a beautiful evening, a group of children were playing on the beach. Suddenly there appeared a middle-aged woman who looked poor and dirty and wore ragged clothes. She appeared to be out of her mind. As she was walking on the beach, she was picking up things and putting them into a bag. The parents warned the children to keep away from her. However, as she passed by them, she smiled at the parents and waved her hands toward the children, but they did not care to return her greeting. Later, they learned that this poor woman was picking up the broken glass and the shells on the beach so that the children playing there would be safe and not harmed. This is true love for others that promotes the cycle of compassionate actions. In today's Gospel text Jesus teaches, "Love your enemies and pray for those who persecute you" (Mt 5: 44). This is one of the most celebrated and oft-quoted texts in Scripture. If we follow this teaching of Jesus, it would seem that we would soon become doormats, letting others walk over us while never reacting or hitting back. But this is not the intention of Jesus' teaching. In a biblical understanding, love involves actions of compassion toward another person and desiring for the well-being of that person because he or she is regarded as God's beloved child.

By such actions of graciousness and kindness toward others, one has to break the cycles of violence and replace them with the cycles of justice and compassion. Therefore, Jesus says, "You have heard that it was said, 'You shall love your neighbor and hate your enemy.' But I say to you, love your enemies, and pray for those who persecute you, that you may be children of your heavenly Father" (Mt 5: 43-45). Here Jesus advises the disciples to resist the evildoers, not by the same violent tactics as their oppressors but with love and compassion. In this way they are to prove their identity as children of the heavenly Father who follows this same technique toward us. "He makes his sun rise on the bad and the good, and causes the rain to fall on the just and the unjust" (v. 45b). God as our compassionate Father does not show partiality. He sets no bounds on His love for us. In the same measure, we are to follow our heavenly Father in practicing love for others while setting no limits. Israel was called to belong to God and live their covenant obligation by walking in God's ways, following the commandments faithfully, and listening to God's voice (cf. Deut 26: 17). Similarly, if we are to prove our identity as God's children, our love must be sincere, generous, unlimited and ever forgiving, because we are to be compassionate as God our heavenly Father is compassionate (cf. Mt 5: 48). This is God's divine method in dealing with us despite our weakness and sinfulness. Do I understand the meaning of this divine technique? How do I treat those who hurt or harm me: with loving compassion or hatred?

Wisdom from St. Francis de Sales: In fact, there is no other art than to set ourselves to the work of loving God, applying ourselves to the practice of those things that are pleasing to him. This is the only means of finding and acquiring this holy love, provided that this practice is undertaken in simplicity, without trouble or solicitude. Simplicity embraces all the means that are prescribed to each of us, according to his vocation, for acquiring the love of God, so that it desires no other motive for acquiring or being incited to the quest for this love than itself. The virtue of simplicity concerns the pure love of God which is its single and only aim (St. Francis de Sales, *The Art of Loving God,* 108).

Prayer: Dear Jesus, thank you for loving and forgiving me despite my sinfulness. Help me to break the cycle of violence by generously practicing compassion, even to those who offend me.

Second Week

Transforming Life

Monday of the Second Week of Lent

Dan 9: 4b-10; Lk 6: 36-38

Preparation: Take a few minutes of silence, setting aside all your worries and anxieties, and become aware of the divine presence.

Listening to God's Word: Stop judging and you will not be judged. Stop condemning and you will not be condemned. Forgive and you will be forgiven. Give and gifts will be given to you; a good measure, packed together, shaken down, and overflowing, will be poured into your lap. For the measure with which you measure will in return be measured out to you (Lk 6: 37-38).

The New Rule of Life

Our life experiences teach us that it is very difficult to be merciful, forgiving, and nonjudgmental. It happens to all of us in the every day events of our life. Whether it is about food, television programs, politics, religious matters, social events, Church teachings, people's actions and attitudes, etc., our natural tendency is to judge them subjectively. As we heard from the Gospel narrative today, Jesus teaches us, "Be merciful, just as also your Father is merciful. Stop judging and you will not be judged. Stop condemning and you will not be condemned. Forgive and you will be forgiven" (Lk 6: 36-37). Jesus goes right to the root cause of our sins. This is the new rule of life and all of us need very much such a life-enriching wisdom. On the one hand, judging and condemning usually creates tension in the family and community, ruins healthy relationships, and causes hostility, hatred, and enmity. On the other hand, being merciful and forgiving generously heals wounded hearts and binds broken relationships, brings joy and peace among people, and inspires them to find the goodness in others.

We may ask why we should be merciful, forgiving, and nonjudgmental. As found in Jesus' teaching, there are two reasons. First, God shows mercy in our misery and forgives our sins. He does not judge or condemn us for our sinfulness and weaknesses but rather loves and forgives us and offers us an extended time of grace for renewal. As God's renewed children, we are to follow the way of the Father by being merciful and forgiving generously (cf. Lk 6: 38a). Second, we only receive what we have given away in life. Therefore, Jesus proposed this new rule of life for our own good that we will be shown mercy, receive forgiveness from others, and not be judged or condemned. "For the measure with which you measure will in turn be measured out to you" (v. 38b). Thus, following the new rule of life taught by Jesus, the cycle of violence is resisted and goodness is promoted. Nelson Mandela said that our human compassion binds us the one to the other—not in pity or patronizingly, but as human beings who have learnt how to turn our common suffering into hope for the future. As disciples of Jesus, we are to make the arena of conflict, arguments, and divisions in our families and communities into a graced space for love and reconciliation. Am I ready to follow this new rule of life to be merciful as the Father is merciful to me? What is the measuring cup of mercy and forgiveness that I follow? Is it full and overflowing or lacking?

Wisdom from St. Francis de Sales: I beg you never to speak evil of your neighbor or say anything, however little, which could offend him. Nevertheless, one must not approve of the evil, flatter it, or try to cover it up, but—when the welfare of the one of whom one speaks requires it—one must speak with candor and say frankly evil of evil, and blame blamable things; because in doing so, God is glorified. Above all, blame the vice and spare as much as possible the person to whom the vice belongs, all the more so because the goodness of God is so great that a single moment is sufficient for entreating His grace. And who can be sure that the one who yesterday was a sinner, and evil, will be so today? (De Sales, *Thy Will Be Done*, 81).

Prayer: Dear Jesus, thank you for teaching me to be merciful and forgiving. Guide me to follow your new rule of life by practicing mercy toward others and avoiding harsh judgments.

Tuesday of the Second Week of Lent

Is 1: 10, 16-20; Mt 23: 1-12

Preparation: Take a few minutes of silence, setting aside all your worries and anxieties, and become aware of the divine presence.

Listening to God's Word: For they preach but they do not practice. They tie up heavy burdens hard to carry and lay them on people's shoulders, but they will not lift a finger to move them. All their works are performed to be seen. They widen their phylacteries and lengthen their tassels. They love places of honor at banquets, seats of honor in synagogues, greetings in marketplaces, and the salutation 'Rabbi' (Mt 23: 5b-7).

Self-promotion or Selfless Service

In our occupational world today, seeking public acknowledgement and self-promotion has become common features of human life. People advertise themselves to receive promotion, to get a job, or to be praised and honored publicly. They desire the honorable place, to be praised by others, and aspire to be the greatest. But choosing the path of Jesus so as to grow in Christian perfection leads us to foster meekness, humility, and mercy. As we heard in the Gospel text today, Jesus says that, "The greatest among you must be your servant. Whoever exalts himself will be humbled; but whoever humbles himself will be exalted" (Mt 23: 11-12). Leadership in a Christian community must be servant-leadership after the pattern of Jesus himself. Jesus the Son of God became our Savior not by asserting his power and authority for his self-glorification but by dying on the Cross for us. He has shown us an example that as believers we can achieve greatness only by serving one another in love and not by claiming self-promotion through public praise or honorable status.

Mahatma Gandhi, influenced by the teachings of Jesus, resolved to live a life of simplicity and humility. Though he was an erudite person and nationally acclaimed leader of the Indian freedom movement, one day he noticed the poor people in India with the bare minimum of clothing laboring all day under the sun, bearing its heat. From that day he renounced his high-class western dress and began to wear the cotton cloth of his own people. So once someone asked him during his self-imposed silence, "What message can you give for the people?" He passed a note that read, "My life is my message." Promoting self interests separates and devalues people. Serving others selflessly binds people in love, affirms others' worth, and promotes common interests. It is easy to mess up things in life by seeking out self-interest, but it takes time and effort to set things right. Today God invites us to set things right in our faith life by putting away our misdeeds, ceasing to do evil, learning to do good, hearing the cry of the poor, and defending the rights of the powerless (cf. Is 1: 16-17). As followers of Jesus, we are urged today to serve one another in our communities unobserved, without fanfare and adulation. As people in leadership roles and with responsibilities, we are to seek opportunities not for promoting our self-interests but to serve and care for each other in true love. In exercising my leadership roles and daily responsibilities, do I aspire for self-promotion or do I find opportunities to serve others in love? Do I humble or exalt myself in my relationship with others?

Wisdom from St. Francis de Sales: Self-love can be mortified in us, but still it never dies; indeed from time to time and on different occasions, it produces shoots in us, which show that although cut off, it is not rooted out. This is why we do not have the consolation that we ought to have when we see others do well. For what we do not see in ourselves is not so agreeable to us; and what we do see in ourselves is very sweet to us, because we love ourselves tenderly and amorously. But if we had true charity, which makes us have one same heart and one same soul with our neighbor, we should be perfectly filled with consolation when our neighbor did well (De Sales, *Thy Will Be Done*, 191-192).

Prayer: Dear Jesus, thank for your self-abasement to give me new life. Help me to avoid promoting my selfish interests and seeking public honors so that I may appreciate others' giftedness.

Wednesday of the Second Week of Lent

Jer 18: 18-20; Mt 20: 17-28

Preparation: Take a few minutes of silence, setting aside all your worries and anxieties, and become aware of the divine presence.

Listening to God's Word: He said to her, "What do you wish?" She answered him, "Command that these two sons of mine sit, one at your right and the other at your left, in your kingdom." Jesus said in reply, "You do not know what you are asking. Can you drink the cup that I am going to drink?" They said to him, "We can." He replied, "My cup you will indeed drink, but to sit at my right and at my left, this is not mine to give but is for those for whom it has been prepared by my Father" (Mt 20: 21-23).

Drinking from the Cup of Jesus

As the Gospel account today tells us, Jesus and the disciples had contrasting opinions about their journeying toward Jerusalem. Jesus, thinking about His upcoming gruesome death, revealed that He would suffer at the hands of the elders and the religious leaders and die (cf. Mt 20: 18-19), whereas the disciples must have thought that Jesus would claim His position of authority and power in Jerusalem. So they were jarringly arguing about the place of honor at the side of Jesus. According to the ancient customs at table and other special occasions, the most important person was seated in the center, the next most important person was seated at his right, and the third most important person was seated at his left. This is the honorary position that the mother of James and John requested from Jesus (cf. Mt 20: 20-21; in Mark 10: 35-45 the disciples ambitiously argue about it). However, Jesus soberly talked to them about "the cup," and so He asked them, "Can you drink the cup that I am going to drink?" They said to Him, "We can" (Mt 20: 22). While Jesus was thinking and talking about the cup of His suffering and death in Jerusalem, the disciples were imagining the cup of joy in the messianic kingdom. In this light, the biblical image of "the cup" means suffering and death.

This idea was prominent among the prophets to describe the destruction of Jerusalem and the exilic experience of Israel in the year 6 BC (cf. Jer 25: 15, 49: 12; Ez 23: 32-33; Is 51: 17). Jesus used this image of the cup at the last supper (cf. Mt 26: 27) and at Gethsemane (cf. Mk 14: 36). By drinking the cup of suffering and death, Jesus gave Himself up as a ransom to redeem humanity. Prophet Jeremiah too had to drink the cup of suffering for speaking truthfully God's word to the people (cf. Jer 18: 18). Moreover, the image of the cup also leads us to understand the significance of the Eucharist in our life. The cup we share everyday at the table of the Lord is the cup of Jesus' Passion and death. Therefore, our faith-filled experience of drinking from the cup of Jesus urges the believers to follow the footstep of the Master, not for seeking honorific titles and self-acclaiming public status, but to serve and help each other. Jesus himself has set the example as He has come not to be served but to serve and give Himself as a ransom for many (cf. Mt 20: 28). Rejecting the cup of His suffering, that is, refusing to follow the path of Jesus is to reject the cup of His glory. Jesus promises that at His banquet table, only those who suffer and face hardships in following Him faithfully, without experiencing adulation, will sit with Jesus taking the place of honor. Am I ready to drink from the cup of Jesus by following His footsteps in faithfulness even in trials? As I walk to participate in the Eucharistic banquet of Jesus, where do I like to sit? Can I take a few minutes to talk to Him about it today?

Wisdom from St. Francis de Sales: It is the truth that nothing is more capable of giving us a more profound tranquility in this world than often to behold our Lord in all the afflictions that happened to Him from His birth to His death. We shall see there such a sea of contempt and insults, of poverty and indigence, of objections, of pains, of torments, of nakedness, of injuries, and of all sorts of bitterness that in comparison with it we shall know that we are wrong when we call our little mishaps by the names of afflictions, pains, and contradictions since a single little drop of modesty is enough for bearing these things well (De Sales, *Thy Will Be Done*, 155).

Prayer: Dear Jesus, thank you for restoring me to eternal life by your suffering and passion. Motivate me to endure the suffering to follow you in fidelity through my self-emptiness.

Thursday of the Second Week of Lent

Jer 17: 5-10; Lk 16: 19-31

Preparation: Take a few minutes of silence, setting aside all your worries and anxieties, and become aware of the divine presence.

Listening to God's Word: Abraham replied, "My child, remember that you received what was good during your lifetime while Lazarus likewise received what was bad; but now he is comforted here, whereas you are tormented. Moreover, between us and you a great chasm is established to prevent anyone from crossing who might wish to go from our side to yours or from your side to ours" (Lk 16: 25-26).

The Lasting Chasm

Once, a young man was sharing his experience of saving an elderly man who decided to end his life by suicide. It was because the elderly person was physically handicapped, and having been abandoned by his family he became homeless. He also in the course of time suffered painful sores in one of his legs. As he could not take care himself and no one helped him, his sores became so deep and severe that worms formed in his leg. Unable to face this suffering and the shame of abandonment by society, he decided to commit suicide. It was at this moment that the young man happened to see him suffering illness and abandoned. The young man volunteered to help him and he spent his own money for the treatment. He himself cleaned and bandaged the soars, removing about two pounds of worms from his leg. Finally, the elderly person was admitted into a government hospital and was treated. Now he is fully cured of his illness and lives happily in good health. He appreciates with gratitude the kindness of that young man. If the young man had not paid attention to that elderly man lying on the road side and been sensitive to his suffering, he would have killed himself. One moment of compassionate listening and little acts of kindness to those who suffer can bring hope to them, save their life, and open up new opportunities for a happy life. However, attitudes of indifference and non-sensitivity to people's needs create a living hell which will be the lasting chasm that torments human life.

The Gospel parable of Jesus about the rich man and the poor Lazarus is a concrete illustration of the consequence of such a lasting chasm. The poor man must have been lying at the gate of the rich man's house for a long time. The description of Lazarus' suffering that the dogs used to lick his sores explains the wretchedness of his living conditions (cf. Lk 16: 21). The rich man must have passed by Lazarus every day but did not pay attention to his suffering nor did he hear his cry for life. It seems to be that Lazarus was a non-person to the rich man who was concerned only about himself and enjoying the luxuries of life. He already created in this world a deep chasm between himself and others around him by his attitudes of indifference and non-sensitivity, especially toward the suffering and less fortunate people. That chasm continued to exist for him even after death. Both of them reaped what they sowed during their life on earth. Lazarus endured the suffering of this life by trusting in God alone and he received the blessings of eternal happiness at the bosom of Abraham (v. 22), whereas the rich man, because of his selfishness and uncaring attitude toward his suffering brothers and sisters around him, received the torment of suffering after his death (v. 23). The parable teaches us that there will be a reversal of things in God's kingdom. The final judgment about us is of our own making (cf. Jer 17: 5-7). Even today in our world, such a deep chasm is created among people by the attitudes of indifference, greed, and non-sensitivity to the cries of the poor. Do I create or break the lasting chasm in my family and communities? Do I hear Jesus inviting me to listen to the cries of the poor and the suffering and bring them hope by deeds of love?

Wisdom from St. Francis de Sales: Jesus Christ Himself said, "Love one another. Such as my love has been for you, so must your love be for each other" (Jn 13:34). You must give a lot of thought to this statement, because it means that we must love others more than we love ourselves. The Lord always put others before Himself and still continues to do that, making Himself our food every time we receive Him in the Blessed Sacrament. In like manner He wants us to love others and even to prefer our neighbor to ourselves (De Sales, *Spiritual Treatise IV,* from *Every Day with SFS,* 298).

Prayer: Dear Jesus, thank you for removing the chasm that alienates people in our society. Lead me to break the walls of separation by having a loving concern and care for those in need.

Friday of the Second Week of Lent

Gen 37: 3-4, 12-13, 17-28; Mt 21: 33-43, 45-46

Preparation: Take a few minutes of silence, setting aside all your worries and anxieties, and become aware of the divine presence.

Listening to God's Word: Finally, he sent his son to them, thinking, "They will respect my son." But when the tenants saw the son, they said to one another, "This is the heir. Come, let us kill him and acquire his inheritance." They seized him, threw him out of the vineyard, and killed him (Mt 21: 37-39).

The Rejected Cornerstone

The building experts rejected a piece of stone unworthy to be in the position of prominence in constructing a building. But the same stone had been used by the same experts as the most prominent stone in the same structure. This allegory had been used by the Psalmist (Ps 118) to refer to the unlikely choice of David as the king by Yahweh or his continuous victory as the king of Israel. In either case, Yahweh played a crucial role in raising David from his lowly state as a shepherd to be a king and endowing him with many victories. This Psalm is also used to recall the humble origin of Jesus from a poor family in Nazareth to be the Messiah but rejected by the religious leaders of his time (cf. Mt 21: 42). In this context, the parable of the vineyard and the tenants is used by the early Church to explain the rejection of Jesus. Moreover, the parable also reflects the social custom of first century Palestine where the land owner would lease out his farms and vineyards to sharecroppers (tenants). The tenant farmers would cultivate the land in exchange for a certain amount of fees or for a percentage of the produce, but the major portion of the profit belonged to the land owner. Therefore, at the appropriate time of the harvest, the land owner would send his agents to collect what was owed to him. But as narrated in the parable, the tenant farmers planned to cheat the owner and inherit his vineyard. Thus, they violated the contract and proved to be unfaithful to the land owner. They tortured and killed the agents of the owner and finally his only son (cf. Mt 21: 42) with the intention of misappropriating the owner's property. Finally, the tenants had to face the consequences of their own acts of injustice and disloyalty.

Rejection of the just ones has been part of salvation history. The sons of Jacob hated and rejected their brother Joseph (cf. Gen 37: 19-20, 27-28), but finally it was Joseph who became their savior during the time of famine and starvation. Though the people rejected Jesus and His revelation of the Father, He has become by His death and resurrection the way to salvation. Therefore, our rejection of Jesus, the cornerstone of our faith life, as irrelevant and unimportant will result in facing the consequence of rejection by God. Furthermore, we can notice also in our families and society that talented people and those with a disability or have special needs are rejected and neglected on various grounds as irrelevant and unimportant. If opportunities are given, such people will prove to be the most valuable and prominent of persons. They will be able to move groups or families forward and achieve great success. God can do great things even with our littleness. What is my experience? Am I a rejected stone or do I strive to be the most prominent cornerstone? How do I treat people—reject them as unimportant and useless or value them as the most important cornerstone by affirming and appreciating their giftedness?

Wisdom from St. Francis de Sales: Dead faith resembles a dry tree that has no living substance at all. In springtime when other trees bud forth leaves and flowers, this one brings forth nothing, because it does not have sap. It may look like the other trees, to be sure, but it is dead, for it never brings either flowers or fruit. Similarly, dead faith may indeed appear to be living faith, but with this important difference: it bears neither the flowers nor the fruit of good works. Thus, we know by the works which charity performs whether faith is dead or dying. When it produces no good works we conclude that it is dead, and when they are few and sluggish, then it is dying (Visitation, *The Sermons of SFS for Lent*, 37).

Prayer: Loving Jesus, thank you for being the cornerstone of our human salvation. Guide me to see the positive side of people that I may become the cornerstone for their growth.

Saturday of the Second Week of Lent

Mic 7: 14-15, 18-20; Lk 15: 1-3, 11-32

Preparation: Take a few minutes of silence, setting aside all your worries and anxieties, and become aware of the divine presence.

Listening to God's Word: Coming to his senses he thought, "How many of my father's hired workers have more than enough food to eat, but here am I, dying from hunger. I shall get up and go to my father and I shall say to him, 'Father, I have sinned against heaven and against you. I no longer deserve to be called your son; treat me as you would treat one of your hired workers.'" So he got up and went back to his father (Lk 15: 17-20).

Home-coming to the Father

Since our family is very important to us, we dearly love our family members. Do you have the experience of dealing with a wayward member of your family? If you thought about one such experience while reading this story of the prodigal son, where do you find yourself? The context of the story is that the religious leaders complained about Jesus' acceptance of sinners (Lk 15: 1-2). This is in fact a wonderful masterpiece of an inspirational story about the sinner's homecoming to the Father. Returning back home to the Lord is a joyful experience of communal celebration. It is a life-transforming experience of light in darkness and joy in sadness. The way the story is narrated we can notice that the emphasis is not on who commits sin but what happens after committing sin. Home-coming to the Lord with repentance involves the process of self-awareness, decision-making, and consequently the experience of healing and restoration. This process is obviously seen in the youngest son's effort to come back home to his father. Coming to himself amidst misfortunes, he became aware of his sinfulness and mistakes that caused his utter misery (v. 17). The only real failure is the one from which we learn nothing. So his self-awareness was a moment of enlightenment to accept his present condition of brokenness and wretchedness.

The young man in the story was not hooked up with the errors and failures of his past but learned from them and decided to restart his life. Such a positive learning from his own sinfulness created in him a deep sense of confidence and trust in his father's generous love. So he said with determination, "I will get up and go to my father" (Lk 15: 18). Consequently, he resolved to give up his former way of life and accept the new life of grace. For this new life of repentance and forgiveness, the young man was ready to accept whatever might happen—shame, guilt, and perhaps rejection. However, what happened in reality was beyond his expectation and imagination. While recognizing the son coming back home, the father did not wait passively. He ran out to meet him on the way (v. 20c). He embraced him and hugged him; even before the son expressed his repentance, the father recognized him as his son and began to celebrate with the whole family (v. 22-24). The super abundance of the father's love in action brought the son comfort and consolation, forgiveness of sins, and healing from wounds inflicted by shame and guilt. Jesus tells us that God is like that father. That the way He accepts and welcomes us back home is by loving and forgiving us unconditionally despite our sinfulness. We are valuable and precious in the eyes of God who as a merciful Father will find us sooner or later. Lent is the special time to celebrate our homecoming to the Father. Do I know that Jesus is seeking after me and that the Father is anxiously waiting for my return with outstretched arms? Can I take the first step this Lent to rise up from my misery and come home to the Father?

Wisdom from St. Francis de Sales: The secret of regaining all the time lost through sin is to be found in the tears you shed for your sins; not tears of the eyes, for God does not ask that of everybody; but tears of the heart, tears of repentance, of the broken and contrite heart. Bathe all that part of you, which has remained dry and desiccated with these invisible tears. Open your heart to love and love will come and plunge you into its refreshing waters of life. Who knows if, in the sight of God, all these past years spent in the wilderness will not be transformed into a pool of living waters, making your heart a fertile land of delights (Joseph Tissot, *The Art of Utilizing our Faults,* 180-181).

Prayer: Loving Jesus, thank you for revealing the nature of the Father's love. Help me to rise up and come back to the Father in repentance and that I would offer the same forgiveness for others.

Third Week

Growing in Complete Faith

Monday of the Third Week of Lent

2Kgs 5: 1-15b; Lk 4: 24-30

Preparation: Take a few minutes of silence, setting aside all your worries and anxieties, and become aware of the divine presence.

Listening to God's Word: When the people in the synagogue heard this, they were all filled with fury. They rose up, drove him out of the town, and led him to the brow of the hill of which their town had been built, to hurl him down headlong. But he passed through the midst of them and went away (Lk 4: 28-30).

Accepting God on His Terms

The experience of rejection by one's family and native people is very painful. Jesus also had discouraging moments from the beginning to the end of his ministry. The Gospel narrative today provides Jesus' first experience of rejection by his native people. When Jesus proclaimed and explained about the fulfillment of God's Word, the people at the synagogue were excited and appreciated Him: "All spoke highly of him and were amazed at the gracious words that came from his mouth" (Lk 4: 22). But then, within a short while, they became outraged and turned against Jesus to the extent of hurling him down from the hill (v. 29-30). Why such a harsh reaction? It is because of Jesus' revelation that God's gift of salvation is not restricted to a particular group of people alone. As a free gift, it is extended to all who can accept it in faith on God's own terms. To substantiate his teaching, Jesus referred to the ministry of the prophets Elijah and Elisha where the widow of Zarephath and Naaman, the Syrian official, accepted the teaching of the prophets and believed in the grace of God. This is what the people at Nazareth could not accept from Jesus. They only understood God's promises of messianic blessings on their own terms of expectation, and they believed as God's chosen people that only they had the right to claim access to God's gift of salvation. The non-Jews (Gentiles) could not have access to it because they did not belong to the covenant people of Israel. It was the first time they heard a Jewish teacher speaking about God's visitation to non-Jews outside the boundaries of Israel the covenant community.

The widow of Zarephath obeyed Elijah's words by faith in God's grace and consequently she was protected from severe famine and drought (cf. 1Kg 17: 8-10). Even Naaman expected God's grace to occur on human terms with an extraordinary healing miracle. So he refused to dip himself into the river. But once he did accept Elisha's words on God's own terms, he experienced healing of his disease and confessed, "Now I know that there is no God in all the earth, except in Israel" (2Kg 5: 15). It happens to us also. When we merely understand God's free gift of love and blessings in terms of our own expectations, we will end up experiencing discouragement, unanswered prayers, and the silence of God. But when we come to God with openness and accept everything in terms of His plan, we will experience God's nearness enriching our life with many blessings. If we are going to approach others' actions and reactions toward us from our own expectations of subjective view points, we will surely go through rejection-experiences in life. How do I approach God during this Lent—according to my own expectations or on God's own terms? Do I exclude people because they do not belong to my circle, or do I welcome and reach out to them in love going outside of my boundaries?

Wisdom from St. Francis de Sales: Here is the most important point: find out what God wants, and when you know, try to carry it out cheerfully or at least courageously; not only that, but you must love this will of God and the obligations it entails, even if it means performing the most menial tasks in the world the rest of your life, because whatever sauce God chooses for us, it should be all the same to us. In this practice lies the very bull's-eye of perfection at which we must all aim, and whoever comes nearest to it wins the prize. But be of good heart, I beg you; little by little train your will to follow God's will, wherever it may lead you; see that your will is strongly roused when your conscience says: God wants this (Thibert, *Letters of Spiritual Direction,* 109).

Prayer: Dear Jesus, thank you for revealing God's gift of salvation that embraces everyone. Help me to accept God's blessings according to His purpose and not project my own motives.

Tuesday of the Third Week of Lent

Dan 3: 25-34; Mt 18: 21-35

Preparation: Take a few minutes of silence, setting aside all your worries and anxieties, and become aware of the divine presence.

Listening to God's Word: Moved with compassion the master of that servant let him go and forgave him the loan. When that servant had left, he found one of his fellow servants who owed him a much smaller amount. He seized him and started to choke him, demanding "Pay back what you owe" (Mt 18: 27-28).

Forgiveness—A Human Necessity

The situations of human life today remind us that forgiveness is one of our most basic human needs when facing the cycle of hatred, enmity, revenge, retaliation, and violence in society. But our experiences teach us that it is difficult to offer and receive forgiveness. Yet, Jesus shows by His example that forgiveness, though difficult, is possible. The parable of the unforgiving servant succinctly illustrates our everyday petition in the Lord's Prayer: "Forgive us our debts as we forgive our debtors" (Mt 6: 12). Through this parable, Jesus teaches us to practice wholehearted and limitless forgiveness: "Not seven times but seventy-seven times" (Mt 18: 22). Why should we forgive without limit? There are two reasons. First, we have already received unconditional forgiveness and love from God. The only response He asks of us for this free gift is to extend wholehearted forgiveness to others. So St. Paul exhorts us, "Forgive one another as God has forgiven you in Christ" (Eph 4: 32). This must be the true character of Jesus' disciples. Hence, since God has reconciled us to Himself through Christ and has entrusted to us the message of reconciliation (cf. 2Cor 5: 18-19), we are called to be peace makers (cf. Mt 5: 9) and ministers of reconciliation. But we do not always do it. The master in the parable having compassion for the servant had forgiven his debts but the servant in turn refused to forgive his fellow servant (cf. Mt 18: 28-30). This shows that as humans we are mistake makers and prone to error. Therefore, we are ourselves in need of forgiveness. This brings us to the second reason that forgiving others without limit is a practical way to break the cycle of injury and retaliation.

More often our experiences of pain and hurt blind us so that we want those who do us harm to suffer in the same measure. If our attitude of revenge provokes us to retaliation, it shows that we conveniently forget God's generously offered forgiveness. Consequently, the cycle of injury for injury, pain for pain keeps escalating. Therefore, Jesus proposes a radical way of refusing to hurt others back by offering forgiveness. This is the only possible way to break the cycle of revenge and violence in our families and society, because love recreates, repentance renews, and forgiveness heals and restores broken relationships. Therefore, the necessity for unlimited forgiveness is to offer the offending party another chance of grace for renewal. But it demands a lot from us—seventy times seven is an infinite number. "Forgiveness is the name of love practiced among people who love poorly. The hard truth is that all people love poorly. We need to forgive and be forgiven every day, every hour increasingly. That is the great work of love among the fellowship of the weak that is the human family" (Henri Nouwen). Am I ready to forgive others generously in my family and work place? Do I escalate injury and retaliation by refusing to forgive, or do I make efforts to break the cycle of vengeance and violence by refusing to hit back?

Wisdom from St. Francis de Sales: How displeasing to God are rash judgments! The judgments of the children of men are rash because they are not judges of one another. In judging they take over the function of our Lord. They are rash because the principal malice of sin depends on the intention and consent of the heart. So that we ourselves may not be judged, we should not judge others but judge ourselves. While our Lord forbids the one, the apostle commands the other saying: if we judge ourselves we will not be judged (1Cor 11:31). But, we do exactly the opposite. Indeed we do not stop doing what is forbidden to us by judging our neighbor at every turn, and never do what is enjoined on us—to judge ourselves (De Sales, *IDL,* Ch. 28, 248-249).

Prayer: Dear Jesus, thank you for your generosity in forgiving me by dying on the Cross. Grant me the grace to be generous in forgiving others without limit and thus to be a peace maker.

Wednesday of the Third Week of Lent

Deut 4: 1, 5-9; Mt 5: 17-19

Preparation: Take a few minutes of silence, setting aside all your worries and anxieties, and become aware of the divine presence.

Listening to God's Word: Therefore, whoever breaks one of the least of these commandments and teaches others to do so will be called least in the kingdom of heaven. But whoever obeys and teaches these commandments will be called greatest in the kingdom of heaven. I tell you, unless your righteousness surpasses that of the scribes and Pharisees, you will not enter into the kingdom of heaven (Mt 5: 19-20).

Obeying God's Commandments

There are basic laws and rules for every society, religion, and institution. The main focus of such laws is to bring orderliness, assure the safety of people, protect the individual and common interests, and ensure a system of fairness and smooth functioning. When people break these laws, due punishment is imposed to remind them and others the importance of obeying the laws and rules to safeguard public and individual interests. In the religious life, there is a higher insistence on "obedience" to one's superiors and to the constitutional requirements of a particular Order. Obedience is one of the three vows (the other two are chastity and poverty) men and women religious profess to follow in their life. The Scripture too speaks about obedience to God's commandments. Moses taught the people, "Now, Israel, hear the statutes and decrees which I am teaching you to observe, that you may live, and may enter in and take possession of the land which the Lord, the God of your fathers, is giving you" (Deut 4: 1). The commandments were the guiding principles for the people of Israel to live faithfully as the covenant people of God. Jesus teaches, "Whoever obeys and teaches these commandments will be called greatest in the kingdom of heaven" (Mt 5: 19b). Now we may ask, what is the meaning of obedience?

The English word "obedience" comes from the Latin phrase *ob audire* which means to listen with great attention. Hence, obedience literally means listening (cf. Henri M. Nouwen, *From Fear to Love,* 11). It is a willingness to listen to each another, listen to what God says to us through the people around us, and listen to what the circumstances and our living environments are demanding from us. Therefore, a life of obedience is a life in which we are listening. Jesus taught and interpreted the Law and the prophets in a way that saved and enriched people's lives, bringing them God's blessings. It is said that there are two kinds of people, namely, anchors and motors. The anchors are the pessimists who would tie us to our past. Such people find fault with everyone and everything. They judge, complain, accuse, criticize, blame, and pull us down. For them there is no forward movement for growth. They are like those who are stuck literally with the letters of the law and the commandments. The other group is the motors who are optimists. They are positive, creative, appreciative, inspiring, and uplifting in their attitudes and approaches. They remind us of our energy and strength, encouraging us to learn from our mistakes and pursue our dreams and goals despite failures (cf. Joseph F. Sica, *Living with Passion,* 23). Jesus acted like a motor when interpreting and keeping the Law. We must choose to be a motor and not an anchor when following God's commandments so that we will be creative in our thinking and positive in our attitudes and be the greatest in God's kingdom. What is my understanding of obeying God's commandments? Do I choose to be an anchor, discouraging and criticizing others, or do I strive to be a motor, inspiring and appreciating people?

Wisdom from St. Francis de Sales: Obey God's known will and his good pleasure. In order to practice self-abandonment, we must obey the known will of God, and also the will of his good pleasure: the one by resignation and the other by indifference. The known will of God includes his commandments, his counsels, his inspirations, and the guidance of our spiritual directors. God's will of good pleasure concerns events that we cannot foresee (De Sales, *The Art of Loving God,* 14-15).

Prayer: Loving Jesus, thank you for teaching me God's commandments as life-giving. Help me to follow you by listening to your word and obeying God's commandments in spirit and truth.

Thursday of the Third Week of Lent

Jer 7: 23-28; Lk 11: 14-23

Preparation: Take a few minutes of silence, setting aside all your worries and anxieties, and become aware of the divine presence.

Listening to God's Word: He was driving out a demon that was mute, and when the demon had gone out, the mute person spoke and the crowds were amazed. Some of them said, "By the power of Beelzebul, the prince of demons, he drives out demons." Others, to test him, asked him for a sign from heaven (Lk 11: 14-16).

With Him or Against Him

The miracles of Jesus—either healing from diseases or driving out the evil spirits—always created mixed reactions from the people: amazement (Lk 11: 14), fear (9: 43), doubt (4: 36) and faith (5: 26), and some even demanded further signs (11: 16). But Jesus never performed a miracle for convincing the people of his power and authority. He did everything to fulfill the purpose of God's plan, that is, human salvation. In the first-century Mediterranean world, people believed that God's divine power was breaking in and, consequently, the appearance of many wonderworkers was common. In this context, the question of Jesus' audience was not "How did He do that?" but "By whose power did He do that?" So, some of the people accused Jesus of driving out the demons by the power of Beelzebul, the prince of demons. This disdainful name for Satan seems to be derived from "Baal-zebub" which means "lord of the flies," a Philistine deity (cf. 2Kgs 1: 2). Jesus' response to this accusation was that if his deeds could destroy the power of Satan, then he was not using the power of Satan but rather "the finger of God." This is an allusion to the presence of God's reign which restores people to wholeness and overcomes the powers of evil.

These works of healing diseases and destroying the powers of Satan are the signs of the Messianic age unfolded through Jesus. The appropriate response must be to accept Jesus in faith and believe in the power of God revealed through Him. Therefore, Jesus said, "Whoever is not with me is against me, and whoever does not gather with me scatters" (Lk 11: 23). The idea of "gathering with me" means the joining of people in faith around Jesus in order to follow His way of life. When we realize the presence of God's kingdom within us and rejoice over it, we will know that Jesus will live in us as our Lord and Savior. We will experience inner peace and happiness. But unfortunately, we often fail to do this as we seek after many other things in life apart from God. As the prophet Jeremiah preached, Israel too failed to listen to God's voice. They walked in the hardness of their evil hearts turning their back to God (cf. Jer 24). The audience of Jesus too doubted his power and refused to believe in Him. But Jesus revealed that by refusing to believe and accept His revelation of God's reign, we get divided, scattered, and confused. During this Lent, Jesus invites us to be with Him and walk with Him in our faith life so that we can gather around Him to experience the messianic blessings of healing, joy, peace, and contentment. In my decisions and actions, am I with Jesus or against Him? Do I walk with Jesus and experience His life-redeeming power, especially in moments of struggle and troubles, or do I get scattered from Him in discouragement and anguish?

Wisdom from St. Francis de Sales: There are still other matters where without doubt God's will is seen, such as trials, illnesses and chronic conditions. That is why we should accept them with a good heart, and conform our will to that of God who permits them. Anyone who can arrive at the point of not only supporting them patiently but even of willing them, that person can be said to have acquired a great conformity. Thus, the death of relatives, various losses, illnesses, dryness or distractions in prayer—these give us opportunities to grow in perfection (Thibert, *Letters of Spiritual Direction*, 105).

Prayer: Dear Jesus, thank you for overcoming the powers of evil. Guide me with your Spirit to walk with you in trust and confidence that I will experience your blessings in all moments of life.

Friday of the Third Week of Lent

Hosea 14: 2-10; Mk 12: 28-34

Preparation: Take a few minutes of silence, setting aside all your worries and anxieties, and become aware of the divine presence.

Listening to God's Word: Jesus replied, "The first is this: 'Hear, O Israel! The Lord our God is Lord alone! You shall love the Lord your God with all your heart, with all your soul, with all your mind, and with all your strength.' The second is this: 'You shall love your neighbor as yourself.' There is no other commandment greater than these" (Mk 12: 29-31).

Loving is Difficult but Worth Doing

Blessed Teresa of Calcutta says, "To love and to be loved, we must know our brothers and sisters. For knowledge always leads to love, and love in action is service to everyone in need. Spread love everywhere you go: first of all in your own house. Give love to your children, to your wife or husband, to a next door neighbor. Let no one ever come to you without leaving better and happier. Be the living expression of God's kindness; kindness in your face, kindness in your eyes, kindness in your smile, kindness in your warm greeting." As we heard in the Gospel narrative today, a scribe as a learned man came forward to consult with Jesus about the one greatest commandment. He was not trying to know if there are only a few commandments that are to be followed and others to be discarded. Rather, he was trying to find out whether Jesus could sum up the entire Torah into a single statement. Jesus responded, "The first is this: 'Hear, O Israel! You shall love the Lord your God with all your heart, with all your soul, with all your mind and with all your strength.'" (Mk 12: 29-30). This is the traditional Jewish Shema prayer from Deut 6: 4-9 that has to be recited twice a day by every faithful Jew. He added, "The second is this: 'You shall love your neighbor as yourself'" (v. 31). This is from the Holiness Code of Israel (cf. Lev 19: 18). Accordingly, the people of Israel understood a neighbor as referring to their own fellow Jew and as a member of their covenant community.

Thus, Jesus summed up the entire Torah into one commandment of loving God and one's neighbor. There is nothing greater than this. The heart (*kardia*) is the seat of all human emotions, the soul (*psyche*) is the center of human vitality and consciousness, and the strength (*ischys*) denotes human power or might (cf. Barbara E. Reid, *Daily Reflections for Lent 2007*, 34). Thus, the whole human person with one's faculties must love God. In the same manner, one should love one's neighbor as oneself. This is the most difficult thing to practice. As the prophet Hosea cried out, the people of Israel deliberately failed to live by this love commandment and they collapsed through their sins and guilt. So the prophet admonished them to return back to the Lord asking for God's forgiveness that they would blossom forth again (cf. Hose 14: 2-6). From our own daily experiences, we know that all of us do very well in loving ourselves but most of the time loving God with our whole person is an overwhelming challenge. Still harder is to value and love our neighbors as ourselves. That is why Jesus places the commandment of loving God and neighbor on the same scale, because he teaches us that the way to know how we love God is to love our neighbors as ourselves. During this Lent let me ask myself, what makes loving God and neighbor easier or more difficult for me? How do I strive to love others in truthfulness even if it is challenging?

Wisdom from St. Francis de Sales: Children who have a good father (mother) ought to imitate him (her) and follow his (her) commandments in all things. Now we have a Father better than all others and from whom all good is derived (Jas 1:17). His commandments can be nothing but perfect and salutary. Thus, we should imitate Him as perfectly as possible, and also obey His divine ordinances. But of all His precepts, there is none which He stresses so earnestly as that of the love of neighbor. Let us love then to the whole extent of our hearts, in order to please our heavenly Father, but let us love reasonably; that is, let our love be guided by reason, which desires that we love the soul of the neighbor more than his body. But let us love his body also, and then, in proper order, all that pertains to the neighbor (Visitation, *The Sermons of SFS for Lent*, 96).

Prayer: Dear Jesus, thank you for your unconditional love for me. Grant me your grace to love you and my brothers and sisters with a sincere heart in order to express your love for the world.

Saturday of the Third Week of Lent

Hosea 6: 1-6; Lk 18: 9-14

Preparation: Take a few minutes of silence, setting aside all your worries and anxieties, and become aware of the divine presence.

Listening to God's Word: The Pharisee took up his position and spoke this prayer to himself, "O God, I thank you that I am not like the rest of humanity—greedy, dishonest, adulterous—or even like this tax collector. I fast twice a week, and I pay tithes on my whole income." But the tax collector stood off at a distance and would not even raise his eyes to heaven but beat his breast and prayed, "O God, be merciful to me a sinner" (Lk 18: 11- 13).

The Danger of Self-righteousness

We normally expect people to be upright and righteous, but no one likes the attitudes of pride and self-glorification, harsh judgment, and condemnation that characterize the self-righteous. Self-righteousness reflects "better-than-thou attitudes" which often destroy one's relationship with God and others. Why was the Pharisee, in spite of his religiosity and good works, not acceptable before God? As we heard in the Gospel text, the content of his prayer was self-glorification before God. First, he said that he was not like the rest of others—greedy, dishonest, adulterous, or even like the tax collector (cf. Lk 18: 11). Secondly, he boasted that he fasted twice a week and paid tithes on his income (v. 12). By proclaiming his acts of self-righteousness, the Pharisee presented himself as better than others. He was standing before God like an already-filled vessel. There was no more space in him for God's grace. So he went home unjustified. The Sage says, "Entrust your works to the Lord, and your plans will succeed" (Prov 16: 3). If the good deeds are done to affirm one's self-righteousness like the self-glorified Pharisee, it will displease the Lord.

But the tax collector stood before God with the attitude of humility and sincere contrition (v. 13). Despite his social stigma as an outcast, he must have done some good deeds for others. In his prayer he did not focus on whatever he did. He did not despise the rest of people by comparing himself with them. He only came before God examining himself whether his attitudes and actions offended and wounded others. He realized his human shortcomings and so he prayed for God's mercy (v. 13b). The tax collector stood before God like an empty vessel and God filled him with His grace of love and forgiveness. The Apostle Peter says, "God opposes the proud but bestows favor on the humble" (1 Pet 5: 5). Through this parable the evangelist highlights that prayer is faith in action. It is not an optional exercise to demonstrate one's relationship with God but prayer itself is that relationship. Prayer focused on fulfilling our selfish interests is not acceptable before God. As the Lord says through the Prophet, "Your piety is like a morning cloud, like the dew that early passes away" (Hosea 6: 4b). Selfish motives and self-glorification will make our prayers and good works unacceptable before God and others. Therefore, what prevents God's righteousness from responding to our prayers is our self-righteousness. The Sage says, "Every proud man is an abomination to the Lord" (Prov 16: 5). For this reason the Pharisee went home empty-handed and the tax collector went home justified. What is my attitude when coming before God in prayer—self-glorification or self-humiliation? How do I relate with people around me—with self-righteous attitudes or people-oriented love?

Wisdom from St. Francis de Sales: To help you be vigilant in prayer, remind yourself that the graces and benefits of prayer are not like water welling up from the earth, but more like water coming down from heaven; therefore, all our efforts cannot produce them, though it is true that we must ready ourselves to receive them with great care, yet humble and peacefully. We must keep our hearts open and wait for the heavenly dew to fall. Never forget to carry this thought in prayer (Thibert, *Letters of Spiritual Direction*, 100).

Prayer: Loving Jesus, thank you for teaching me to have the right intention in my prayer. Help me to overcome my self-righteousness that I may offer my prayers with sincerity and integrity of heart.

Fourth Week

Moving Toward the Light

Monday of the Fourth Week of Lent

Is 65: 17-21; Jn 4: 43-54

Preparation: Take a few minutes of silence, setting aside all your worries and anxieties, and become aware of the divine presence.

Listening to God's Word: The royal official said to him, "Sir, come down before my child dies." Jesus said to him, "You may go; your son will live." The man believed what Jesus said to him and left. While he was on his way back, his slaves met him and told him that his boy would live (Jn 4: 49-51).

Hope-assuring Words

We experience helplessness and frustration in varying degrees from different circumstances such as the loss of our dear ones in the family, constant problems, crisis in one's marriage and personal life, suffering chronic illness, unexpected failures, the struggle against injustice and oppression, etc. In facing such events, we might see only hopelessness and darkness around, and we become startled, frightened, and thrown into despair. We might ask in such situations, "What is God doing? Where is God's hand in all this?" However, the Gospel text about the faith experience of the royal official illustrates that Jesus comes to us even in the worst situations with His life-giving and hope-assuring words. The official came to Jesus with desperation as his son was near death (cf. Jn 4: 46-47). He came with a firm belief that Jesus could restore his son to wholeness of health. Jesus said to him, "You may go; your son will live" (v. 50a). Here the word "to live" is used with a double meaning: first, to recover from illness, and second, to receive new life through faith in Jesus. The official unconditionally believed the words of Jesus. His faith was rewarded and his son lived (v. 50-51). Jesus' words changed impending death into new life, sorrow into gladness, and doubt into hope.

Isaiah spoke hope-assuring words of God's promise about a new creation for the people of Israel. The people who lost their temple, had their land invaded, houses destroyed, and suffered exile in a foreign land heard the prophet speak words of comfort that God would bring them back to their homeland (cf. Is 65: 17). There would be no more crying or weeping but only rejoicing and gladness (v. 18-20). These words of the prophet Isaiah portray that Yahweh is neither silent nor indifferent to the cries and sorrows of Israel. He is actively involved in their life and committed to bringing them lasting peace, joy, and prosperity in their homeland. That is the new creation Israel will experience. The people believed the prophet's words of hope and encouragement and began a new life by returning to their homeland under God's protection. In the same way and in our times of sorrow and pain, discouragement and despair, and pain from hurts and wounds, Jesus' words come to us as words of healing, encouragement, and challenge. We must be ready to welcome Him in faith and trust in His promise of hope for a new creation. "I have become my own version of an optimist. If I can't make it through one door, I'll go through another door or I'll make a door. Something terrific will come no matter how dark the present" (Rabindranath Tagore). Whenever I read or listen to God's word from the Scripture, do I welcome it in faith as hope-assuring and life-promising words? Do I speak and share with people around me words of appreciation, compassion, and motivation, or do I speak words that cause pain, hurt, and discouragement?

Wisdom from St. Francis de Sales: You should never get discouraged. All that you are expected to do is to have a courage that is gentle and patient and take your time and all the care needed to heal and comfort your heart in the wake of the assaults it has endured. Have courage. Let us do our best, all we possibly can, and God will be happy with us. Have you ever seen people discharge a fire arm or shoot with a rifle? They often fall flat on the ground; so, too, those who learn the art of riding a horse; but they do not for that matter think that they're in any way defeated. It is one thing sometimes to be beaten, and quite another thing to be vanquished (Tissot, *The Art of Utilizing our Faults According to SFS,* 47, 48).

Prayer: Dear Jesus, thank you for your life-promising words. Help me in my faith journey to believe in your words and walk by your words that I may speak words of encouragement.

Tuesday of the Fourth Week of Lent

Ezek 47: 1-9; Jn 5: 1-16

Preparation: Take a few minutes of silence, setting aside all your worries and anxieties, and become aware of the divine presence.

Listening to God's Word: When Jesus saw him lying there and knew that he had been ill for a long time, he said to him, "Do you want to be well?" The sick man answered him, "Sir, I have no one to put me into the pool when the water is stirred up; while I am on my way, someone else gets down there before me." Jesus said to him, "Rise, take up your mat, and walk." Immediately the man became well, took up his mat, and walked (Jn 5: 6-9).

Healing Grace

The Gospel story of Jesus healing a sick man at the pool of Bethesda is a dramatic illustration that God does not give up on us. As the narrative presents, the man was suffering a physical illness for thirty-eight years (Jn 5: 5). He seems to have been suffering a physical disability as he was unable to rush into the water before the others (v. 7). His relatives and friends seemed to have given up on him, probably after trying all those years to help him. The man's desperate attempt to dip himself into the pool shows that he had not given up trying. At any case, the sick person was in a hopeless condition of life and was experiencing abandonment and rejection by everyone. Moreover, he was lying at the pool for many long years without attracting anyone's attention until he was found by Jesus. After he was healed and became part of society, he was the point of everyone's attention and became the issue of controversy (v. 10ff). However, when Jesus saw the suffering man, He did not distance Himself but drew closer to him recognizing his need for healing. Therefore, he asked, "Do you want to be well?" (v. 6). The man had to respond immediately or else he would regret it later. So he did respond to Jesus, saying, "I have no one to put me into the pool when the water is stirred up" (v. 7a). As if saying to the man, "Do not worry, I am here for you," Jesus said to him, "Rise, take up your mat, and walk" (v. 8) and immediately the man became well and went home rejoicing.

While everyone there distanced themselves from the suffering man and neglected him, Jesus paid attention to his suffering and brought him healing of wholeness. His own people had given up on him but Jesus did not. Jesus took the first initiative and restored him to good health. This is how God is dealing with every one of us. We may be tormented by our daily problems, struggles, trials, and anxieties. We may be over-burdened by dark moments of despair, discouragement, failures, and personal weaknesses. In these moments, we might give up on ourselves and not even recognize Jesus' presence. But He finds us with our pain and problems and asks us, "Do you want to be healed?" If we do not respond to Him at that moment in faith asking for His grace, we may have to regret it later. God's healing grace is gratuitous and unearned. God sees our human condition and in His mercy God takes the initiative to reach out to us in our need (v. 6a; cf. Lk 15: 1-30). Like the river of living water that offers life to all living creatures (cf. Ez 47: 9), God's healing grace flows into our life through Jesus to give us new life. We cannot escape from God's sight for He knows our going in and coming out. Wherever, we go, He is there (cf. Ps 139: 1-2, 7-12). How do I respond to Jesus' initiative to bring me physical and spiritual healing? Do I really want to be healed of my self-indulgence and selfishness? Like Jesus, do I pay attention to the needs and pains of others? Do I reach out to mend people's hurts and wounds by offering words of motivation and deeds of kindness?

Wisdom from St. Francis de Sales: Oh, what a good sign it is for a Christian to take pleasure in listening to God's word (Jn 8:47) and to leave all to follow Him! So long as we have a care for ourselves, I mean a care full of anxiety, our Lord permits us to act; but when we abandon all to Him, He takes a tender care of us, and His Providence for us is great or small according to the measure of our abandonment (Visitation, *The Sermons of SFS for Lent,* 118).

Prayer: Dear Jesus, thank you for your blessings that come as a soothing ointment for me. Inspire me to seek your grace that I may be healed, strengthened, and motivated in life.

Wednesday of the Fourth Week of Lent

Is 49: 8-15; Jn 5: 17-30

Preparation: Take a few minutes of silence, setting aside all your worries and anxieties, and become aware of the divine presence.

Listening to God's Word: But Jesus answered them, "My Father is at work until now, so I am at work." For this reason the Jews tried all the more to kill him, because he not only broke the Sabbath but he also called God his own father, making himself equal to God. Jesus answered and said to them, "Amen, amen, I say to you, a son cannot do anything on his own, but only what he sees his father doing; for what he does, his son will do also" (Jn 5: 17).

The Father's Work

The Gospel account as proclaimed today is the response of Jesus for the double charges He faced during His ministry. What were the charges? Breaking the Sabbath by healing a paralyzed person (cf. Jn 5: 15-16) and making Himself equal with God by calling Him as His Father (cf. v. 18b). Both these actions were serious sins of blasphemy according to the Jews. Why did Jesus do this? It is to continue the work of the Father. So Jesus said, "My Father is at work until now, so I am at work" (v. 17). We may ask then what the work of the Father is. It is transmitting life to humanity: "For just as the Father raises the dead and gives life, so also the son gives life to whomever he wishes" (v. 21). The Jews believed that though God rested on the Sabbath (seventh) day after creation, He actually never rests from His work of giving life to creation, because if God rests from His work, creation itself would cease to exist. In the same way, Jesus as the Son of God cannot do otherwise except doing what the Father is doing. Jesus proved His defense on the ground of God's action of giving life. There is nothing that can prevent Him from doing the Father's work of on-going creation because this is the mission of Jesus as the Son. All those who believe in Jesus and follow Him will share in His work of transmitting life.

Whatever Jesus said and did was to remember the Father's work of transmitting life to the world. To "remember" in the biblical sense means to "make present" as in the last supper where Jesus said to the disciples, "Do this in memory (remembrance) of me" (Lk 22: 19). In the Eucharist, we remember (make present) Jesus' sacrifice at Calvary. As Isaiah says, "The Lord comforts his people and shows mercy to his afflicted" (Is 49: 13). When things go badly in life, when we are afflicted and suffering misfortunes, God the Father remembers us and Jesus comes as our light to give us new life. When Israel lost everything and went into exile, they asked, "Is our God with us? Does God remember us or has he forsaken us?" To them God said, "Can a mother forget her infant, be without tenderness for the child of her womb? Even should she forget, I will never forget you. See, upon the palms of my hands I have written your name" (vv. 14-16). As children of the Father, all of us are to continue His work of transmitting life. In the most troubled moments of our life, we may wonder like the Israelites whether God remembers us. Even if we do not believe in God's love and life-giving presence, it is there. Our loving Father cannot forget us. He remembers us in our troubles. He creates and nurtures us in Jesus to have life. How do I fulfill the Father's work in my life? Is there anything in my life that prevents me from participating in the work of the Father? During this Lent, can I ask Jesus how He wants me to do the Father's work within my own living situations?

Wisdom from St. Francis de Sales: Live entirely for God, and since you have to take part in conversations and social gatherings, try to be of some use to others. Do not think that God is further away from you when you are in the midst of the busyness to which your vocation calls you than he would be if you were enjoying a tranquil life (Thibert, *Golden Counsels of SFS*, 12-13).

Prayer: Loving Jesus, thank you for fulfilling the Father's work of giving life to humanity. Help me to follow your example to do the Father's work of affirming and promoting life.

Thursday of the Fourth Week of Lent

Ex 32: 7-14; Jn 5: 31-47

Preparation: Take a few minutes of silence, setting aside all your worries and anxieties, and become aware of the divine presence.

Listening to God's Word: I came in the name of my Father, but you do not accept me; yet if another comes in his own name, you will accept him. How can you believe, when you accept praise from one another and do not seek the praise that comes from the only God? Do not think that I will accuse you before the Father: one who will accuse you is Moses, in whom you have placed your hope (Jn 5: 41-45).

No Accusation

The habit of accusation is the strongest manifestation of pessimistic attitudes and a negative approach toward life and people. So we normally don't like to be around those who accuse or complain a lot. We would like to avoid or limit our contact with such people because accusation hurts and breaks relationships, and complaining is contagious as it causes irritation and unhappiness among people. As we heard in the Gospel today, the religious leaders accused Jesus of violating their religious traditions of observing the Sabbath and of speaking blasphemy by calling God His Father. Jesus did not accuse and condemn them in return (cf. Jn 5: 45) but provided His own actions as a testimony to defend His identity and mission (v. 36). In the Jewish traditions, it was not enough for the accused to prove the truth of certain facts, but also trustworthy witnesses must be brought forward. So, Jesus provided His own actions of giving life as a trustworthy witness that the Father has sent Him. The purpose of His testimony was to evoke a strong faith response from the people including his accusers that they might come to believe in Him and be saved (v. 34, cf. 3: 16-18). According to John, not believing in Jesus is the sin. Therefore, the theme that runs through the testimony of Jesus is life. As His accusers refused to believe in Him, Jesus said, "But you do not want to come to me to have life" (v. 40). Here Jesus presents before us two choices: choosing life by believing in Him or sin by not believing.

We notice in the life of Israel the tendency to accuse and complain. Forgetting God's marvelous way of delivering them from Egypt, the people in the desert turned out to be unfaithful by complaining against God and accusing Moses of abandoning them. So they made a golden calf as their god (cf. Ex 32: 1-4). It would happen to us too. When we face troubled moments or are struggling to find solutions for family and personal issues and problems, we would accuse and complain against God and other people while expressing our anger and frustration. Though God was angry about the people's complaining and accusations, at the pleading of Moses He relented in the punishment He had threatened to inflict on them (vv. 9-10, 14). This expresses vividly the character of God who in His graciousness and love forgives, saves, and gives us life in fullness. This is the work Jesus as the Savior of the world accomplished in His life even by breaking the Sabbath law. He does not condemn or destroy us but offers us opportunities of grace and blessings that we would be saved by believing in Him. What is my faith response to God—accusation and complaining or accepting Jesus and following Him in faithfulness? Do I own responsibility for my wrong decisions and actions or accuse those around me? During this Lent, let me listen to Jesus and ask Him for inspiration and guidance.

Wisdom from St. Francis de Sales: Everyone dislikes reproof, even the saints. When all is said and done, there is no one who does not dislike reproof. What right do we have to be surprised at finding ourselves quick to anger, and ready to resent reproof and contradiction? We must follow the example of the saints who instantly conquered themselves by having recourse to prayer or by humbly asking pardon. Therefore, when administering reproof, be forbearing for it is painful to anyone to be reproved (De Sales, *The Art of Loving God*, 79-81).

Prayer: Dear Jesus, thank you for saving me from sin and death. Grant me your grace to avoid making accusations against you and others that I may learn to have a positive approach toward life's realities.

Friday of the Fourth Week of Lent

Wis 2: 1, 12-22; Jn 7: 1-2, 10, 25-30

Preparation: Take a few minutes of silence, setting aside all your worries and anxieties, and become aware of the divine presence.

Listening to God's Word: So some of the inhabitants of Jerusalem said, "Is he not the one they are trying to kill? And look, he is speaking openly and they say nothing to him. Could the authorities have realized that he is the Messiah? But we know where he is from. When the Messiah comes, no one will know where he is from" (Jn 7: 25-27).

Trust Him or Test Him

As we come closer to the end of the Lenten season, the Liturgy of the Word in the coming weeks will prepare us for the final, climatic events of Holy Week. In the Liturgy of the Word today, we learn how bad people seek to prey on good people. Evil moved by intolerance attempts to eliminate the good, and the unjust, in condemnation, tries to inflict death on the just. The Gospel account presents that during His ministry Jesus always struggled to prove His identity as the Son of God. Many people refused to believe in Him because of His claim to identify Himself with God, as it was a blasphemy according to the Jews to compare oneself with God. Moreover, there was a popular belief among them that the Messiah would suddenly manifest one day and bring about a sudden change. Until then He would be hidden and unknown, whereas people knew the origin and the family background of Jesus (cf. Jn 7: 26-27). That is why the people demanded from Jesus a public manifestation to prove Him to the world (v. 4). However, though Jesus was well aware of His origin as the Son sent by the Father (cf. v. 28-29), He was always ready to meet only the criteria of His mission entrusted by the Father than fulfilling the criteria of the people's expectation. That was the reason He refused to manifest His power for the sake of convincing His audience. In the Old Testament, Yahweh struggled with the unfaithfulness of Israel, and in the New Testament Jesus was struggling against people's unbelief.

The Sage in the book of Wisdom speaks about how the evil ones taunt the just by accusing and reproaching, reviling and torturing, shaming and condemning, and inflicting pain and death. The unjust cry out that if the just one is truly righteous let God defend and protect him (cf. Wis 2: 12-20). Jesus too faced such situations where His opponents plotted to do away with Him. Life for Jesus indeed became precarious. Demand for a public demonstration of Jesus' power and authority was a continued temptation He faced till His death. There was division among the people—those who believed in Jesus on the basis of the signs He worked, and those who made attempts against His life as they considered Him to be a trouble maker. Which group do we belong to? Our refusal to believe and accept Jesus and His teachings means not knowing the one true God who has sent Jesus to save the world. In our life journey, we may face situations to compromise our faith values and avoid God in life. We may experience continued temptation to make decisions or do things contrary to the Gospel values and our conscience. In such moments, this Lent invites us to make a choice: to trust Him or test Him. How do I respond to Jesus while facing life-challenges—with faithfulness or disloyalty? Do I continue to trust Him despite the struggles that might come, or do I keep testing Him by my unbelief?

Wisdom from St. Francis de Sales: How happy we shall be if we love this divine Goodness that has prepared such favors and blessings for us! Let us all belong to God in the midst of so much busyness brought on by the diversity of worldly things. Where could we give better witness to our fidelity than in the midst of things going wrong? Ah, solitude has its assaults, the world its busyness; in either place we must be courageous, since in either place divine help is available to those who trust in God and who humbly and gently beg for His fatherly assistance (Visitation, *Letters of Spiritual Direction,* 163).

Prayer: Dear Jesus, thank you for fulfilling the Father's purpose of human salvation. Grant me the grace to believe and accept you as my Savior that I will never test you by my unbelief.

Saturday of the Fourth Week of Lent

Jer 11: 18-20; Jn 7: 40-53

Preparation: Take a few minutes of silence, setting aside all your worries and anxieties, and become aware of the divine presence.

Listening to God's Word: Some in the crowd who heard these words said, "This is truly the Prophet." Others said, "This is the Messiah." But others said, "The Messiah will not come from Galilee, will he? Does not scripture say that the Messiah will be of David's family and come from Bethlehem, the village where David lived?" So a division occurred in the crowd because of him (Jn 7: 40-44).

Intolerance of God's Name

We humans intelligently and prudently justify our actions of intolerance and division. We hold God as the primary reason for such justifications. The Hindu religion promotes division and discrimination among people on the basis of different casts. People of various cast groups grow intolerant of others and engage in killing one another. This ideology of cast discrimination justifies itself on the ground that God created human persons as such. The Muslims refer to their religious teaching as the foundation of their Jihad (fighting) against others to protect their religion. Christians too at times take the extreme position of becoming intolerant toward the opposite views, opinions, and certain faith practices of others (including fellow Christians) under the disguise of being loyal to God by defending their true faith traditions. We see such tendencies from the religious leadership of Jesus' time like the Pharisees and the chief priests who plotted to arrest Jesus and punish (kill) Him (cf. Jn 7: 1, 32). Such intolerant attitudes and actions of violence are not the way and the purpose of God. As we heard from the Gospel account today, Jesus became the victim of the intolerant actions carried out by the religious leaders. The Pharisees and the chief priests sent guards to arrest Jesus in order to punish Him on the accusation that He broke the Sabbath law and claimed equality with God (vv. 45-47).

Like Jesus, prophet Jeremiah suffered the wrath of his own people who tried to kill him because he spoke God's word and warned them about the consequence of punishment for their unfaithfulness (cf. Jer 11: 17-19). While people display great devotion and piety in their religious belief and worship God in extravagance, the same people show attitudes of intolerance and carry out acts of violence against each other. It is a total contradiction to their faith and against God's intention. However, God's voice in defense of His faithful ones comes from an unexpected corner. It may be from little children, from one's own life situations and experiences, or from people unfamiliar. But God definitely comes to save and protect those who walk with Him in fidelity. Some people could not accept Jesus because He was a wandering, self-appointed prophet from a little, unpopular village of Nazareth, and He had good training in carpentry rather than in theological education. How could He speak in God's voice claiming equality with God? Thus refusing to believe in Jesus was their problem. But there were others who recognized Jesus' power and believed in Him (Jn 7: 43). Our personal prejudices and favoritism may keep us blind to see the goodness in others and deaf to hear the cry of the oppressed. Our lack of faith and trust may fail us to recognize God's hand at work and listen to God speaking through Jesus and others. This Lent invites us to be patient toward others and compassionately respect one another. Do I foster intolerance toward others due to prejudice and biased approaches or am I respectful and honorable toward them? Do I listen to Jesus speaking to me this Lent through other people and the events in my life?

Wisdom from St. Francis de Sales: Persevere in overcoming yourself in the little everyday frustrations that bother you; let your best efforts be directed there. God wishes nothing else of you at present, so don't waste time doing anything else. Don't long to be other than what you are, but desire to be thoroughly what you are. Direct your thoughts to being very good at that and to bearing the crosses, little or great, that you will find there. Believe me, this is the most important point in the spiritual life. We all love what is according to our taste; few people like what is according to their duty or to God's liking (Thibert, *Letters of Spiritual Direction*, 112).

Prayer: Dear Jesus, thank you for teaching me about gentleness and compassion. Help me to follow your example in learning to be gentle, merciful, and compassionate toward others.

Fifth Week

Seeking Jesus, the Life

Monday of the Fifth Week of Lent

Dan 13: 1-9, 15-17, 19-30, 33-62; Jn 8: 12-20

Preparation: Take a few minutes of silence, setting aside all your worries and anxieties, and become aware of the divine presence.

Listening to God's Word: Jesus spoke to them again, saying, "I am the light of the world. Whoever follows me will not walk in darkness, but will have the light of life." So the Pharisees said to him, "You testify on your own behalf, so your testimony cannot be verified" (Jn 8: 12-13).

To Follow the Light

One of the Jewish religious feasts was the Feast of Tabernacles. It was a pilgrimage feast and people took a pilgrimage to Jerusalem for the celebration (cf. Ex 23: 16; 34: 22; Lev 8: 14). This feast commemorated the dwelling of the Israelites in the tent during their desert wandering after they left Egypt. While journeying to Jerusalem, people would make huts and would live there during the eight days of celebration. If they could not make the pilgrimage to Jerusalem, they were supposed to set up huts outside their homes and eat their meals and sleep in the huts. It was to recall the wilderness experience of their fore-fathers who were cared for by God, Yahweh (cf. Lev 23: 42-43). During the first seven days of celebration, the symbols of water and light and the early morning profession of faith in the one true God occupied a special place. On the final day of the celebration (eighth day), these symbols would be eliminated from the ceremony. It was on this day that Jesus stood up in the temple and proclaimed that He was the living water (cf. Jn 7: 37-38) and the light of the world (cf. 8: 12; 19: 5). In this way, Jesus perfected the symbols of God's gift of water from the well of the Torah and dispelled the darkness of the world as the true light fulfilling the Tabernacle's joy.

Light also is understood as the symbol expressing the presence of God or God's word. The fourth evangelist gives this symbol a new meaning by identifying it with God's revelation in Jesus. Therefore, light and life are the two ways (cf. Jn 1: 4) in which the divine Word expresses itself in the world. In these two ways, humanity experiences the relationship with Jesus the incarnate Word. Thus, the presence of Jesus as the light of the world presents humanity with two crucial choices: to follow Him and have the light of life or to walk in darkness (cf. 8: 12b; cf. 3: 19-21; 12: 35-36). According to John, "to follow" as the language of discipleship involves recognition of Jesus and responding in faithfulness to His offer of life (cf. 10: 27-28). As narrated in the first reading, Susanna remained loyal to God even in trouble, and God enlightened and stirred up Daniel to defend her by right judgment (cf. Dan 13: 44-49). But the religious leaders in today's Gospel account instead of believing and accepting Jesus as the light were debating with Him about His origin and relationship with the Father. However, we must believe that Jesus, as the light in our faith journey, lifts up our spirit, enlightens us with wisdom to make right decisions, inspires us to nurture positive attitudes toward life, and opens our hearts and minds to see good and beauty around us. We must be able to discover the light in others and get connected to people in order to spread the warmth of Jesus' light to everyone around us. When I face the most difficult times and moments of darkness in life, do I seek the light of Jesus to guide me through? Do I recognize the light of Jesus within me and make it shine forth in my family and community? In what ways do I help others to discover the light of Jesus in them and make it shine?

Wisdom from St. Francis de Sales: Observe how kind Divine Providence is to us! God encourages us to have confidence in Him. A son will never perish while he is in the arms of his Almighty Father. If God does not always give us what we ask, He only does this to keep us near Him. He wants us to ask Him for help, storming heaven with a loving violence. He is kind and merciful. As soon as we submit ourselves to His will, He immediately grants our wishes (De Sales, *Letters*, 1513, from *Every Day with SFS*, 90).

Prayer: Loving Jesus, thank you for becoming the light of our world. Help me to accept you as the light of my life, especially in difficult times, and see your light shining forth through others.

Tuesday of the Fifth Week of Lent

Num 21: 4-9; Jn 8: 21-30

Preparation: Take a few minutes of silence, setting aside all your worries and anxieties, and become aware of the divine presence.

Listening to God's Word: He said to them, "You belong to what is below, I belong to what is above. You belong to this world, but I do not belong to this world. That is why I told you that you will die in your sins. If you do not believe that I AM, you will die in your sins." So they said to him, "Who are you?" Jesus said to them, "What I told you from the beginning" (Jn 8: 23-25).

Not Belonging to the World

Our experience tells us that this world is real, endowed with wonders, and our life in this world is very precious. God has given us the opportunity in this world to live our life in its fullness. However, as we heard in the Gospel narrative today in speaking about His departure to the Father, Jesus said, "You belong to what is below, I belong to what is above. You belong to this world, but I do not belong to this world" (Jn 8: 23). What does Jesus mean by this belonging and not belonging to the world? In the understanding of John, though the noun "world" is used neutrally to highlight God's created order where God's revelation through Jesus is available, it is also used to represent what is opposed to God's presence and His redemptive work in Jesus (cf. 15: 19). Thus, the world is used as an image to highlight the contrast between the community of Jesus' disciples and the world. In this light, belonging and not belonging to this world refers to the place of origin for Jesus and the Jewish leaders. As Jesus came from above by the Father's initiative and belonged to the heavenly world, after fulfilling the Father's work of human redemption, He returned to the Father as was His destiny (v. 21, 29). The religious leaders born of this world by human initiative belonged to this world, entangled with all its allurements, attachments, pleasures, and pain. So they belong to what is below, that is, this world alienated from God by rejecting Jesus' revelation of the Father.

Though the disciples live in this world facing its hatred and oppositions, yet they did not belong to the world because of their belief in Jesus and rather belonged to the Father. But people like the religious leaders who did not accept Jesus as the Son of God would suffer the influence of their sin, that is, their sin of unbelief (v. 24). Israel also lost their faith in God's power as they became dismayed and their patience wore out due to lack of food and water on their desert journey (cf. Num 21: 4-5). However, just as they looked at the bronze serpent and lived by God's mercy (v. 9), there is still hope for those who do not believe in Jesus. If they accept His revelation of the Father available in this world and believe in Him, they would belong to the Father and live by Him (Jn 8: 24b). At times this seems to be the case for us too. Although we are very much involved in this world by experiencing its marvelous beauty, rich blessings, and amazing wonders, yet, we face its challenges, trials, crisis, pain, and struggles. In all such experiences, if we believe in Jesus like the first disciples we will belong to the Father and see the hand of God guiding us. Do I belong to Jesus by believing in Him, or do I belong to the world attracted by its material allurements? Do I create a sense of belongingness in my families and faith communities by my compassionate approach toward other members? During this Lent can I spend some time with Jesus and ask for His help to believe in Him always and belong to Him in all moments?

Wisdom from St. Francis de Sales: There is a real temptation to become dissatisfied with the world and depressed about it when we must be in it. God's providence is wiser than we are. We imagine we would feel better if we were on another ship; that may be, but only if we change ourselves! I am the sworn enemy of all those useless, dangerous, unwise desires, for even if what we desire is good, the desiring itself is pointless since God does not want that kind of good for us, but another, toward which he expects us to strive. He might wish to speak to us from the thorny bush as he did to Moses (Ex 3:2), when we expect him to speak to us from the gentle breeze as he did to Elijah (Thibert, *Letters of Spiritual Direction*, 162).

Prayer: Loving Jesus, thank you for reminding me of my identity as God's child. Help me to belong to you and not to this world that I truly follow you, overcoming the forces of this world.

Wednesday of the Fifth Week of Lent

Dan 3: 14-20, 91-92, 95; Jn 8: 31-42

Preparation: Take a few minutes of silence, setting aside all your worries and anxieties, and become aware of the divine presence.

Listening to God's Word: Jesus then said to those Jews who believed in him, "If you remain in my word, you will truly be my disciples, and you will know the truth, and the truth will set you free." They answered him, "We are descendants of Abraham and have never been enslaved to anyone. How can you say, 'You will become free'?" (Jn 8: 31-33).

To Know the Truth

We all speak about truth, expect people to be truthful regarding what they say and do, and raise a voice against untruth happening around us. Some people, if they are powerful, would think that they can twist and play with words and impress their listeners to believe what they say is correct or truthful. That is not the truth which will set us free. In the Gospel episode we heard today, Jesus said to those who believed in Him, "If you remain in my word you will truly be my disciples, and you will know the truth, and the truth will set you free" (Jn 8: 31-32). When the people replied that they were the descendants of Abraham and were not slaves of anyone, Jesus said, "Everyone who commits sin is a slave of sin" (v. 34). There are two questions in this saying that we should pay attention to: What is the truth that Jesus speaks about? What is the sin that enslaves us? First, the truth Jesus speaks about is the truth He revealed about God the Father as loving and compassionate, gracious and forgiving. It is the truth about Jesus Himself who abides with the Father who had sent Him to redeem the world from sin and death. It is the truth about our new birth as children of a loving Father who has saved us by Jesus' death and resurrection. Therefore, to know the truth means knowing and believing in Jesus and God's gift of salvation through Him. In the biblical meaning, knowing implies a personal relationship.

Through our reciprocal personal relationship with Jesus and by remaining in Him, that is, living by His words, we come to know the truth

He revealed that makes us completely free. Abraham is given as the best example of this uninhibited freedom. By listening to God's voice and discerning to follow God's purpose, he experienced a personal relationship with God. Abraham did everything and faced every life challenge by believing without compromise and faithfully following God in life. So he was totally free as God's servant. This brings us to the second question of what is sin. According to John, rejecting God's revelation in Jesus and refusing to believe in Him is the sin. So Jesus said, "If you remain in my word, you will truly be my disciples" (v. 31), but "You are trying to kill me, because my word has no room among you" (v. 37). This was the sin of the religious leaders. Like Abraham who trusted in God's promise, the three young men believed in the truth about the one true God and refused to follow the untruth of worshiping false gods. Though they were thrown into fire, God protected them. The truth of their faith had set them free (cf. Dan 3: 17-18, 24). Judaism taught that the study of the Law would make people free, but Jesus taught that believing in Him and accepting His revelation of the Father's will gives the power to become God's children (cf. 1: 12-13). As disciples of Jesus, we must learn from the school of Jesus to believe in Him and remain in His words. This will give credibility to our call. In our life, truth seems to be very simple but often we find it to be a hard reality. We have the tendency to define what is truth or untruth to achieve our own personal interests. Do I hold on to the truth, or do I distort it to suit my own needs and plans? Do I remain in truth by believing and following Jesus, or do I live in sin by rejecting Him?

Wisdom from St. Francis de Sales: All are called to perfection. But, in truth, we may well say what is said in the holy Gospel, "Many are called, but the elect are few [Matt 20:16; 22:14]. There are many who aspire to perfection, but few attain it because they do not walk as they should— ardently, yet tranquilly; carefully, but confidently; that is to say, relying more on the divine Goodness and His Providence than upon themselves and their own works. We must be very faithful, but without anxiety or eagerness; we must use the means that are given to us according to our vocation, and then remain in peace concerning all the rest. God will always be attentive to provide us with whatever is necessary (Visitation, *The Sermons of SFS for Lent,* 120).

Prayer: Meek and gentle Jesus, thank you for revealing to me the truth about the Father's love. Guide me to know you, believe in you, and walk with you always to find the way to eternal life.

Thursday of the Fifth Week of Lent

Gen 17: 3-9; Jn 8: 51-59

Preparation: Take a few minutes of silence, setting aside all your worries and anxieties, and become aware of the divine presence.

Listening to God's Word: "Amen, amen, I say to you, whoever keeps my word will never see death." So the Jews said to him, "Now we are sure that you are possessed. Abraham died, as did the prophets, yet you say, 'Whoever keeps my word will never taste death.' Are you greater than our father Abraham, who died? Or the prophets, who died? Who do you make yourself out to be?" (Jn 8: 51-53).

Right Understanding

For most of us, misunderstanding seems to be a lasting problem. We think that we speak well, clearly, distinctly, and honestly with the right choice of words. But we see people misunderstanding us, wrongly interpreting the intention of what we have said. They only hear what they want to hear and what they presume we are saying. At the end, they miss our words and give different meaning to the words we spoke. This happened to Jesus too. As we heard from the Gospel text taken from the eighth chapter of John, Jesus spoke about His identity, His mission, and about the Father with directness, clarity, and truthfulness. Yet, His audience, especially the religious leaders, misunderstood His words, wrongly interpreted the intention of His teachings, and accused Him of speaking against God. As a result, they even attempted to arrest Him and stone Him to death. As we move closer to Holy Week to reflect on Jesus' Passion, the Liturgy of the Word presents a more intense situation between Jesus and the crowd. Today's Gospel account is part of such a tense controversy. When Jesus said, "Whoever keeps my word will never see death" (Jn 8: 51), the crowd reacted harshly, saying, "Now we are sure that you are possessed" (v. 52). This is a very direct attack on Jesus with the intention of demeaning and dishonoring Him.

However, Jesus didn't compromise His view point. The more tense the questioning became, the deeper Jesus explained His divine union with the Father and the gift of life as a result of believing in His words. As a consequence, the crowd attempted to stone Him (v. 59). It is not that He did something wrong or unpardonable. It only reflects how much the crowd misunderstood Jesus' words with a biased attitude and judged Him from their own view point. The right understanding about the identity of Abraham and the identity of Israel as a covenant people rests on their faithfulness to God's covenant which would bring them blessings, prosperity, and land. But sadly, Israel often displayed their disloyalty to God (cf. Gen 17: 5-9). We also at times behave in such a manner of misunderstanding what others said or did to us and judge them harshly with a condemning attitude. We often misinterpret God's word in our life when things don't happen as we expect. Lent invites us to understand and believe that Jesus, as the truth, leads us to the Father; as the way, He guides us to live by the truth; and as the life, He offers us words of hope that help us to overcome even death. Do I believe in the life-giving words of Jesus? How do I understand the meaning of God's words that I hear in the most difficult and challenging moments of my life? Do I speak hope-giving and encouraging words in my relationship with others? Let me speak to Jesus about this and ask for grace and inspiration that my words may be life-enriching and motivational.

Wisdom from St. Francis de Sales: Everyone is obliged to strive for the perfection of Christian life, because our Lord commands that we be perfect (Mt 5:48) and St. Paul says the same (2Cor 13:11). Perfection of Christian life consists in conforming our will to that of our good God, who is the sovereign standard and norm for all actions. So in order to acquire perfection we must always consider and recognize what God's will is in everything that concerns us, so that we can flee what he wants us to avoid and accomplish what he wants us to do (Thibert, *Letters of Spiritual Direction,* 105).

Prayer: Loving Jesus, thank you for understanding me with my weaknesses and shortcomings. Lead me to have a right understanding of my brothers and sisters and discover their goodness.

Friday of the Fifth Week of Lent

Jer 20: 10-13; Jn 10: 31-42

Preparation: Take a few minutes of silence, setting aside all your worries and anxieties, and become aware of the divine presence.

Listening to God's Word: If I do not perform my Father's works, do not believe me; but if I perform them, even if you do not believe me, believe the works, so that you may realize and understand that the Father is in me and I am in the Father (Jn 10: 37-38).

The Divine Oneness

We normally take pride and pleasure in speaking about the rich friendships we foster and cherish with our siblings or friends. We often celebrate that relationship, appreciate it, and if needed, prove it with sufficient evidences. This is what Jesus did as we heard in the Gospel narrative today. Though during His public ministry Jesus had a hard time proving His identity as the Son of God, He continually spoke about His relationship with the Father, affirmed it proudly, and proved it with explicit evidences. The religious leaders could not tolerate Jesus' claim to be equal with God. They tried to stone Him as they understood Jesus' claim as a blasphemous act. The Jews did not expect a Messiah who would claim to replace the Temple, but that is what Jesus did by saying, "The Father and I are one" (Jn 10: 30). For the Jews, the Temple was the physical evidence of their belonging to God and God's belonging to them. As their Temple was desecrated by the Assyrian kings, the feast of the Dedication was a celebration of its re-consecration. The Jewish people believed that God's presence in the Holy Temple was the physical assurance of God's personal presence among them. In this setting, Jesus' union with the Father indicates that God's presence among the people through the Temple was perfected through Him. Therefore, He announced that His teachings and works reveal His oneness with the Father. So He said, "Believe the works, so that you may realize and understand that the Father is in me and I am in the Father" (v. 38). This divine union is the oneness of purpose between the Father and Jesus for human salvation. Hence, the indwelling relationship of God the Father and Jesus is not a metaphysical puzzle but evidence of God's love for the redemption of the world: God sent his only Son that everyone who believes in him might have eternal life (cf. Jn 3: 16-17).

Jesus' divine union with the Father fulfills the Jewish expectation of the pre-existence of the Messiah, and Jesus is that Messiah. He was not the long-awaited political liberator but as a Messiah He is the very power of God on life, death, and judgment. Therefore, believing in Jesus' words and works relates the believers with His indwelling divine union with the Father. The fruit of sharing in Jesus' union of oneness with the Father is that believers get a new identity as God's beloved children. As Jesus remained loyal to the mission of the Father and proved His identity as the Son, the believers too, guided by the Holy Spirit, are called to follow the way of Jesus in faithfulness, despite the struggles and trials, and reveal the Father and Jesus to the world. Belonging to Jesus and faithfully living our identity as God's beloved may be our constant struggle. But we should not give up or fall into despair. Like Jesus, we must remain loyal in doing the work of the Father for the salvation of the world. By our belongingness in union with the Father and Jesus, we can experience God's presence as a mighty champion defending us from terror and dangers (cf. Jer 20: 11). Do I understand my identity as God's beloved by my baptism in Jesus? How do I make present the indwelling oneness of Jesus with the Father in my families and faith communities?

Wisdom from St. Francis de Sales: Total commitment never to abandon God or to forsake his gentle love serves as counterweight to our spirits, to preserve them in holy equanimity in the midst of all the changing circumstances which the conditions of this life bring to them. Bees, when caught in a storm in the fields, take up little stones to keep their balance in the air and not to be easily carried away by the storm. Similarly, we hold on eagerly to the precious love of God by our firm determination. Thus we remain steadfast in the midst of the inconstancy and instability of consolations and afflictions, whether temporal or spiritual, exterior or interior (De Sales, *IDL, Part IV,* Ch. 13, 319-320).

Prayer: Gentle Jesus, thank you for finding solidarity with me in your loving kindness. Help me to appreciate your self-gift that like you I will find solidarity with my brothers and sisters in love.

Saturday of the Fifth Week of Lent

Ez 37: 21-28; Jn 11: 45-56

Preparation: Take a few minutes of silence, setting aside all your worries and anxieties, and become aware of the divine presence.

Listening to God's Word: So the chief priests and the Pharisees convened the Sanhedrin and said, "What are we going to do? This man is performing many signs. If we leave him alone, all will believe in him, and the Romans will come and take away both our land and our nation." But one of them, Caiaphas, who was high priest that year, said to them, "You know nothing, nor do you consider that it is better for you that one man should die instead of the people, that the whole nation may not perish" (Jn 11: 47-50).

A Redemptive Death

In any normal situation of life, there is no reason or occasion for anyone to die for others. However, there are people who would prefer to sacrifice their life for a noble cause even by dying. This is the supreme act of love as shown by Maxmilian Kolbe who volunteered to die in place of his fellow prisoner at Auschwitz. The model for this supreme act of sacrifice in love is the redemptive death of Jesus who died to save us from sin and death, giving us new life. His death is not only for a particular people but to gather into one fold the scattered children of God (cf. Jn 11: 52). Jesus died like a good shepherd would die to save His sheep that all those who believe in Him would become God's children. Thus, Jesus' redemptive death reveals the depth of God's love for the world. Hence, Jesus says, "God so loved the world that he gave his only Son, so that everyone who believes in me might not perish but might have eternal life" (cf. 3: 16). St. Augustine says, "The passion of our Lord and Savior Jesus Christ is the hope of glory and a lesson in patience. He loved us so much that sinless himself, he suffered for us sinners the punishment we deserved for our sins. How then can he fail to give us the reward we deserve for our righteousness, for he is the source of righteousness? Brethren, let us then fearlessly acknowledge, and even openly proclaim that Christ was crucified for us; let us confess it, not in fear but in joy, not in shame but in glory." This must be our belief and duty as followers of Jesus.

The Jews believed that when the high priest asked for God's counsel for the nation, God spoke through him. In this light the words of Caiaphas are to be understood. If the people were stirred up and social unrest was caused by Jesus' teachings and actions, the whole people had to face severe reprisal from the Romans who would go to the extent of destroying the Temple. This would mean destroying their Jewish identity as a nation. So the high priest suggested that it was better to get rid of one person for the sake of saving the whole nation. In first-century Israel, there was a strong idea that a good person might die for the nation and effect God's blessings upon all the people. Ezekiel announced that God would establish one people, one land, one king, and one sanctuary (cf. Ez 37: 21-22). John adds to this prophecy of Ezekiel that Jesus, as the Messiah, would do just that by His death on the Cross to gather into one the children of God who are scattered and dispersed on many grounds (cf. Jn 11: 51-52). How do I understand the meaning of Jesus' death on the Cross? Do I experience the redemptive power of Jesus' death when I come to Him in prayer and in the celebration of the sacraments?

Wisdom from St. Francis de Sales: We must then fear this last passage, but without anxiety or inner disturbance. Let us rather have a fear which keeps us prepared and always ready to die well. And how are we to do that? St. Augustine says, "To die well we must live well." As our life is, so will be our death. So the general rule for a good death is to lead a good life. It is true that even while living well you will fear death, but your fear will be holy and tranquil, relying on the merits of our Lord's passion, without which death would certainly be dreadful and terrifying (Visitation, *The Sermons of SFS for Lent*, 142).

Prayer: Loving Jesus, thank you for dying in order to give me new life. Help me to die to all that is sinful in me that I may become your instrument to bring life-enriching blessings for others.

Holy Week

The Divine Character of Love

Monday of the Sixth Week of Lent

Is 42: 1-7; Jn 12: 1-11

Preparation: Take a few minutes of silence, setting aside all your worries and anxieties, and become aware of the divine presence.

Listening to God's Word: Mary took a liter of costly perfumed oil made from genuine aromatic nard and anointed the feet of Jesus and dried them with her hair; the house was filled with the fragrance of the oil. Then Judas the Iscariot, one of his disciples, and the one who would betray him, said, "Why was this oil not sold for three hundred days' wages and given to the poor?" (Jn 12: 3-5).

Extravagant Love

It is our human nature that we are ready to offer valuable things or do any sacrifice as a sign of our deep love and appreciation for our loved ones. In the Gospel account that we heard today, we see people's responses of true love and also reactions of disgust toward Jesus. The family meal is generally the external sign of celebrating loving friendships and sharing joy with one another. The kind of family meal that Jesus shared in the company of Lazarus, Mary, and Martha was a symbol affirming their true friendship and love. In this family atmosphere of affection and friendship, there were positive responses of affirmation and appreciation. Martha served Jesus, and Mary anointed Him with a costly perfume (cf. Jn 12: 2-3). The fragrance of the perfume signified not only the material element but also affirmed their deep friendship. Mary on her part did something so extravagant to express her love for Jesus, that is, she dried the feet of Jesus with her hair (v. 3b). According to the social custom of the time, no Jewish woman would lose her hair in public because that would be considered immodest and indecent. But Mary did that as a sign of her extravagant love for Jesus.

Surprisingly, there were also reactions from people like Judas Iscariot who criticized such an act of true love (Jn 12: 4-5). Likewise, the religious leaders plotted against Jesus. However, as the prophet Isaiah proclaims, God out of his extravagant love holds us by the hand and sets us as a light to bring total human liberation (cf. Is 42: 6-7). Jesus demonstrated the extravagant love of God for us by enduring death on the Cross like a suffering servant. Jesus' gift of Himself in the Eucharist nourishes our soul and gives us strength in our faith journey. God's graces we receive through the sacraments are like soothing ointment giving us consolation and forgiveness of sins. "What does love look like? It has the hands to help others. It has the feet to hasten to the poor and needy. It has eyes to see misery and want. It has the ears to hear the sighs and sorrows of people. That is what love looks like" (St. Augustine). God's word in the Scripture comes to us as God's assurance of encouragement, hope, and new life. In the same way, people's little acts of goodness and compassion lift up our wavering spirit, motivating us to take a new direction in life. Nevertheless, we often have the tendency to take all such blessings for granted and regard them as something not very special or as unimportant. How do I affirm and appreciate God's love for me? Do I value and honor people's acts of love and kindness even if done in a simple way? In what ways do I express my extravagant love for God and others?

Wisdom from St. Francis de Sales: O God! With how much humility and spiritual abasement ought we to live on this earth! But also what great reason to anchor our hope and confidence completely in our Lord! For if even after having committed sins such as denying Him, persevering and spending one's life in horrible crimes and iniquities, one can find forgiveness when one returns to the Cross to which our redemption is attached (1Cor 1:30), why should a sinner of either kind fear in life and in death to return to God? Ah, let him answer boldly that this God died for all (2Cor 5:15), and that those who look upon the Cross, no matter how sinful they are, will find salvation and redemption (Visitation, *The Sermons of SFS for Lent,* 195-196).

Prayer: Loving Jesus, thank you for enacting in your Passion God's extravagant love. Guide me by your Spirit to walk with you faithfully and, like you, generously love my brothers and sisters.

Tuesday of the Sixth Week of Lent

Is 49: 1-6; Jn 13: 21-33, 36-38

Preparation: Take a few minutes of silence, setting aside all your worries and anxieties, and become aware of the divine presence.

Listening to God's Word: Jesus answered, "It is the one to whom I hand the morsel after I have dipped it." So he dipped the morsel and took it and handed it to Judas, son of Simon the Iscariot. After he took the morsel, Satan entered him. So Jesus said to him, "What you are going to do, do quickly." So he took the morsel and left at once. And it was night (Jn 13: 26-27, 30).

Flight into Darkness

What would be your feeling and expectation if you knew the certainty of your death? Or how would you accept betrayal and abandonment by your own friends and dear ones? Today's Gospel account presents the inner agony of Jesus as He became more and more aware of His own death. After washing the feet of the disciples, Jesus revealed His upcoming death in his farewell discourse. As suffering caused by close friends is very painful, Jesus too suffered due to His disciples' response of unfaithfulness. One disciple betrayed Him, another one denied Him, and others deserted Him in times of danger and trials. As Isaiah said, Jesus was aware that He was sent as a "light of the world to bring God's gift of salvation. So he took refuge in God" (cf. Is 49: 5-6). He glorified the Father through His suffering and death (cf. Jn13: 31-32). Jesus, the light of the world, was going to overcome the darkness of sin and death, whereas, His trusted disciples were moving away from the light into the darkness of confusion, ignorance, and doubt.

Judas, after receiving the morsel of bread, immediately went out in the night (v. 30). As night signifies darkness, he walked away from Jesus the light into the darkness of betraying his Master to those who wanted to kill Him (cf. Jn 8: 12; 12: 35). Peter, deserting Jesus on His arrest, ran for his life and thus moved out into the darkness by denying his teacher. The other disciples abandoned Jesus in His most difficult and challenging moment and thus moved from light into the darkness of doubt, fear, and despair. Similarly, whenever we give the last place for God in our life, we refuse to accept the light. Whenever we deliberately compromise our faith values and disregard the moral principles of justice and truth, we consciously embrace the darkness. Whenever we are focused on our selfish interests and show an uncaring attitude to the cries of the poor, we are moving away from Jesus the light into the darkness of fear, confusion, and unfaithfulness. God says through Isaiah the Prophet, "I will make you a light to the nations that my salvation may reach to the ends of the earth" (Is 49: 6b). Our call is to live as a people of light and not in darkness. Do we understand that our role as disciples of Jesus is to be a light in our world? "Looking at Jesus in his passion, we see humanity's sufferings as well as our personal histories reflected as in a mirror. Although there was no sin in Christ, he took upon himself what man could not endure: injustice, evil, sin, hatred, suffering and finally death" (Pope John Paul II). What is my response to Jesus in my faith life— uncompromising fidelity or refusal and betrayal? In times of hardships and oppositions, do I walk in the light of Jesus or move toward darkness in fear and frustration?

Wisdom from St. Francis de Sales: You say that your powerlessness hurts you greatly for it keeps you from entering into yourself and approaching God. This is wrong, without doubt. God leaves this powerlessness in us for His glory and for our great benefit. He wants our misery to be the throne of His mercy, and our powerlessness the seat of His omnipotence. This powerlessness does not hinder you from entering into yourself, although it does hinder you from growing complacent about yourself. One thing is necessary for us, which is to be with Him. Therefore, love God crucified amid darkness, and stay near Him (De Sales, *Thy Will Be Done,* 142-143).

Prayer: Dear Jesus, thank you for teaching me by your suffering the meaning of faithfulness. Grant me your grace never to desert you but follow your light in fidelity even in hardships.

Wednesday of the Sixth Week of Lent

Is 50: 4-9; Mt 26: 14-25

Preparation: Take a few minutes of silence, setting aside all your worries and anxieties, and become aware of the divine presence.

Listening to God's Word: Then one of the Twelve, who was called Judas Iscariot, went to the chief priests and said, "What are you willing to give me if I hand him over to you?" They paid him thirty pieces of silver, and from that time on he looked for an opportunity to hand him over (Mt 26: 14-16).

Betrayal of Faithfulness

Our life experiences show us that disloyalty and unfaithfulness by a dear friend or one's spouse will hurt very deeply. In this sense, betrayal is the worst action anyone will dare to do because it would destroy every genuine human relationship, preventing people from trusting and believing even those who are honest in their relationship. Jesus too had to face the experience of betrayal in unfaithfulness by one of His own close disciples. But His reaction in such a situation was amazing. He remained serene, peaceful, and confident. Though Jesus knew very well that Judas would show his unfaithfulness by betraying Him, yet He invited him to share His fellowship meal. Thus, by treating the unfaithful disciples with love He challenged them to the demands of discipleship in loyalty. Moreover, Judas too was exposed to the teachings, healing miracles, and the divine revelation of Jesus. He was aware of the challenges and dangers awaiting Jesus in Jerusalem. Yet, he approached the chief priests, "What will you give me if I betray him to you," and they promised him thirty silver coins. So he looked for the opportunity to betray his master (cf. Mt 26: 15-16). This is the most shameful expression of unfaithfulness, the worst face of treachery, and the highest point of selfishness.

By this act of disloyalty, Judas compromised the love of Jesus for him and his privileged place of being Jesus' disciple in God's kingdom. He compromised his trust and allegiance to Jesus who graciously welcomed and accepted him as His own, and he deliberately compromised God's free gift of salvation through Jesus for the sake of valueless material things. Compromising one's conviction and faith values for selfish gain is the worst expression of betrayal. By his act of betraying Jesus' faithfulness, Judas fell from grace. From being an Apostle, he became an apostate and ruined himself. Recognizing in shame his betrayal of faithfulness, he hanged himself (cf. Mt 27: 4). This was the serious sin of Israel against God. They compromised His covenantal love by neglecting and disobeying His commandments. They betrayed God's merciful love in unfaithfulness by worshiping idols. They indeed experienced the consequence of their unfaithfulness and disloyalty by suffering destruction and exile (cf. Is 50: 1), whereas the suffering servant won salvation by his loyalty and faithfulness even in trial and suffering (vv. 5-7). Though the people deserted God by betraying His unconditional love, God remains always faithful and trustworthy. Though many times we betray God's graciousness and loving goodness by our acts of disloyalty and compromising our faith values, He always shows His faithfulness in loving us dearly and passionately. Untruthfulness and betrayal of faithfulness are serious problems in married life and in one's relationships with others. Hence, the challenging question today is, do I remain faithful and grateful to Jesus, or do I betray Him by compromising or giving up my faith conviction for selfish gains? Am I truthful and faithful in my relationships with the people who love me dearly and truly?

Wisdom from St. Francis de Sales: My daughter (son), a heart that greatly esteems and loves Jesus Christ crucified, loves His pains, torments, being spat on, insults, destitutions, hungers, thirsts, ignominies and death. And when some small share of these comes to it, it makes a very jubilee over them for joy, and embraces them amorously. You must then every day make a study of our Lord amid the pains of our redemption, and consider what a blessing it will be to you to share in them. With a great love of the Cross and of the Passion of our Lord, you must cry out with St. Andrew, "O good Cross, so loved by my Savior, when will you receive me into your arms?" (De Sales, *Thy Will Be Done,* 155-156).

Prayer: Dear Jesus, thank you for loving and forgiving me despite my continued failures. Guide me to overcome my temptation to betray your love so that I will remain with you in fidelity.

Holy Thursday
The Mass of the Lord's Supper

Ex 12: 1-8, 11-14; 1Cor 11: 23-26; Jn 13: 1-15

Preparation: Take a few minutes of silence, setting aside all your worries and anxieties, and become aware of the divine presence.

Listening to God's Word: If I, therefore, the master and teacher, have washed your feet, you ought to wash one another's feet. I have given you a model to follow, so that as I have done for you, you should also do. Amen, amen, I say to you, no slave is greater than his master nor any messenger greater than the one who sent him (Jn 13: 14-16).

Self-giving through Loving Service

Today's celebration of the Lord's Supper is a profound symbolic action of God's self-emptiness through Jesus. Washing the feet of someone or serving others is customarily the work of slaves or household servants. However, in washing the feet of His disciples, Jesus assumed the roles of a servant and the host. In a society that highly valued honor and status, Jesus showed His love for others in total contrast to the social custom of His time. "He took off his outer garments" (Jn 13: 4). The outer garment was the symbol of His status as Lord and Teacher and He took it off. He then "took a towel and tied it around his waist" which is usually the gesture of one who is ready to serve. Jesus then poured water into a basin and began to wash the disciples' feet and dry them with the towel (v. 5). This is the work of a slave or a servant. Thus, this symbolic action of Jesus explains His self-gift through His death on the Cross. Moreover, this radical gift of His self-emptiness in love is concretely explained by the Eucharistic imagery. He took the bread, broke it and said, "This is my body that is for you," and He took the cup filled with wine and said, "This cup is the new covenant in my blood" (cf. 1Cor 11: 24-25). The breaking of His body and shedding of His blood is the culmination of His total gift of Himself for us through His death on the Cross. Pope Benedict XVI explains that "Jesus' death on the Cross is the culmination of God's turning against Himself in which He gives Himself in order to save us from sin and death and to raise us up to a life of grace. This is the nature of God's love in its most radical form. Hence, our Eucharistic communion draws us into Jesus' act of self-oblation, that is, we personally enter into the very dynamic of his self-giving" (*Deus Caritas Est*, nos. 12-13). So, St. Paul rightly teaches that "for as often as you eat this bread and drink the cup, you proclaim the death of the Lord until he comes" (1Cor 11: 26).

We celebrate this self-emptiness of Jesus in the foot-washing ceremony and continue to proclaim His death for us in our daily Eucharistic sacrifice. But the Lord's self-gift must be lived out in our daily life through our own acts of self-emptiness and in loving service to one another as a sign of living out our common priesthood. This is the meaning of Jesus' instruction to the disciples, "If I, the master and teacher, have washed your feet, you ought to wash one another's feet" (Jn 13: 14). Nevertheless, as a believing community we would certainly experience a certain kind of struggle in living out the self-emptiness of Jesus. While the forces of the world would pull us away from God, the power of Jesus' love would pull us toward God. When we celebrate Jesus' act of self-emptiness, we have a choice either to embrace Jesus' lifestyle or turn away from Him. Am I ready to enact Jesus' self-gift of love in my own act of self-emptiness in loving service? Today, let me resolve to turn against myself in order to turn toward Him and one another in love so that I can proclaim the death of the Lord Jesus.

Wisdom from St. Francis de Sales: Nothing can disturb us but self-love and the importance we give ourselves. If we are without feelings of tenderness and compassion in our heart, have no delight or devotion in prayer and no interior sweetness in meditation, we fall into sadness; if we have difficulty in doing things well or if something gets in the way of our plans, at once we are anxious to overcome it and fret about getting rid of it. Why all this? Undoubtedly because we love our consolations, our comfort, our convenience. Self-love, then, is one of the sources of our disturbance; the other is the importance we give ourselves (Thibert, *Letters of Spiritual Direction,* 118-119).

Prayer: Loving Jesus, thank you for showing me the power of true love. Help me to follow your example in demonstrating my love for God and neighbor through my self-emptiness.

Good Friday The Lord's Passion

Is 52: 13-53: 12; Heb 4: 14-16, 5: 7-9; Jn 18: 1-19: 42

Preparation: Take a few minutes of silence, setting aside all your worries and anxieties, and become aware of the divine presence.

Listening to God's Word: Then Pilate took Jesus and had him scourged. And the soldiers wove a crown out of thorns and placed it on his head, and clothed him in a purple cloak, and they came to him and said, "Hail, king of the Jews!" And they struck him repeatedly. Once more Pilate went out and said to them, "Look, I am bringing him out to you, so that you may know that I find no guilt in him." So Jesus came out, wearing the crown of thorns and the purple cloak (Jn 19: 1-5).

His Death Saved Us

The acts of torturing, stoning to death, beheading or shooting in order to execute punishment on people for the crimes they've committed are truly the most detestable inhuman actions. Similarly, as we heard in the Passion account, Jesus' death on the Cross is awfully painful and heart-breaking. The suffering He endured is extremely cruel that one is prompted to ask why should Jesus go through such an inhuman death and for what purpose? Jesus truly portrayed through His suffering the God of love and compassion. Hence, Jesus' death on the Cross helps us to understand two things. First, the death of Jesus is the culmination and the concrete expression of God's love for us. Secondly, He made no compromise whatsoever. God said to the people of Israel, "With age-old love I have loved you" (cf. Jer 31: 3a); "because you are precious to my eyes and glorious, I love you" (cf. Is 43: 4a). Jesus' death on the Cross reveals and affirms such an unconditional love. By enduring a cruel death on the Cross, "He bore our infirmities, and endured our sufferings, for our sake he was afflicted. He was pierced for our offences, and crushed for our sins, upon him was the chastisement that makes us whole, by his stripes we were healed" (cf. Is 53: 4-6). He died for you and me that we might live through Him. Do we believe in this redemptive sacrifice of Jesus?

If we look at Jesus crucified and ask Him how much He loves us, He would say in silence, "I stretched out my hands on the Cross to say 'this much' and I died for you." This is the message that challenges us today. As we are healed by His sufferings and restored by His everlasting love, we too must heal others' wounds by forgiving, lessening their burdens with generous giving, and restoring them to a new life by genuine love. In demonstrating His love for us, Jesus did not make any compromise. He always remained faithful to His promise of covenantal love. He could have rejected such a cruel death but He did not. Jesus remains always faithful and trustworthy though at times we are tempted to be unfaithful and disloyal to Him (cf. 1Tim 2: 13). Jesus' final commendation, "Father, it is finished; into your hands, I commend my spirit," explains His faithfulness to the mission entrusted to Him. Even now, whenever we commit the sin of compromising our faith values, we contribute to the Passion of Christ. Unfaithfulness of married couples to their spouses, uncaring attitudes of children toward their parents, and deliberate silence to the cry of marginalized people, are the signs that signify our sin of compromise. As John Chrysostom says, "Cross as the symbol of life is the means of salvation, the source of countless blessings. It delivered us from sin and death. Though we have sinned, yet, it reconciles us with God, has regained his friendship and has brought us back to him. We have discovered a well spring." Do I understand in gratitude the depth of Jesus' love for me? How do I reciprocate this love in my life?

Wisdom from St. Francis de Sales: God could have redeemed us in a thousand other ways than that of His Son's death. But He did not will to do so, for what may have been sufficient for our salvation was not sufficient for His love; and to show us how much He loved us, this divine Son died the cruelest and most ignominious of deaths, that of the Cross. The implication of all this is clear: since He died of love for us, we also should die of love for Him, or if we cannot die of love, at least we should live for Him alone (2Cor 5:14-15). Since He died for us and was lifted up on the Cross, there is no other redemption but in this Cross (Visitation, *The Sermons of SFS for Lent,* 181).

Prayer: Dear Jesus, thank you for the gift of the Cross on which you died for my salvation. Inspire me to keep the Cross in front of me in my faith journey that I will steadfastly follow you.

Holy Saturday The Lord's Resurrection

Mt 28: 1-10 (A); Mk 16: 1-7 (B); Lk 24: 1-12 (C)

Preparation: Take a few minutes of silence, setting aside all your worries and anxieties, and become aware of the divine presence.

Listening to God's Word: But at daybreak on the first day of the week they took the spices they had prepared and went to the tomb. They found the stone rolled away from the tomb; but when they entered, they did not find the body of the Lord Jesus. While they were puzzling over this, behold, two men in dazzling garments appeared to them. They were terrified and bowed their faces to the ground. They said to them, "Why do you seek the living one among the dead? He is not here, but he has been raised" (Lk 24: 1-6).

We are the Resurrection People

The resurrection of Jesus as the greatest of miracles is the basis of our Christian faith. If Jesus is not risen, His birth has no relevance, and our faith has no meaning. There is an ancient story about Joseph of Arimathea, who was a very wealthy Pharisee and an influential member of the council, but a secret follower of Jesus. It was Joseph who went to Pilate and asked for Jesus' body after the crucifixion. And it was Joseph who supplied the tomb for Jesus' burial. It happened that after the burial of Jesus in the tomb, someone pulled him aside and asked, "Joseph, that was such a beautiful, costly, hand-hewn tomb. Why on earth did you give it for burying Jesus?" "Why not? There is no problem at all," Joseph answered. "He only needs it for the weekend." Yes, indeed. Jesus is risen, overcoming the power of sin and death. Therefore, St. Paul teaches us that, "If Christ has not been raised, then empty too is our preaching; empty, too, your faith. And if Christ has not been raised, your faith is vain; you are still in your sins" (1Cor 15: 14, 17). The feast of Jesus' resurrection brings us the joyful message that we are the "resurrection people." This implies that we are not supposed to lie buried in the tomb of our sins, evil habits, and dangerous addictions. As we believe in the risen Jesus, no tomb can hold us down anymore—neither the tomb of despair, discouragement, and doubt, nor death.

The resurrection proves that Jesus is our God who died for us but lives forever. Without the resurrection, Jesus would have remained till today as a righteous person who met a tragic and vulnerable death. As He is risen from death, His resurrection gives us hope and encouragement in our world of sufferings and struggles, sorrows and tears, assuring us of our own resurrection. Our risen Lord reminds us that life is worth living. The real presence of the risen Jesus in our faith life gives meaning to our personal choices, courage in our faith witness, and purpose to our common identity as a renewed people. Therefore, resurrection is the good news of hope for us and alleluia must be our happy song. But we should remember that before we experience resurrection in our lives, we're called to die to sin, die to self and to all that creates hopelessness and lifelessness in our world. The resurrection of Jesus is about our own resurrection and it is about seeing our world in a new way with optimism and hope. Early Sunday morning, Mary did not find what she was looking for—the dead body of Jesus. But she found something better than she could have imagined—the risen Jesus (cf. Lk 24: 5-6). Nothing can curtail the power of Jesus, neither the power of evil nor the power of death. He is risen indeed and thus paved the way for our own resurrection. Do I experience the presence of the risen Jesus in my faith life? Do I become an instrument of resurrection joy for others?

Wisdom from St. Francis de Sales: We must love what God loves. Now, He loves our vocation; so let us also love it, and not occupy ourselves with thinking on that of others. Let us do our duty; each one's cross is not too much for him. Do diligently the service of your vocation, and often recollect yourself, and put yourself in spirit at the feet of our Lord, and say, "My Lord, whether I run or stay, I am all yours and you mine; whatever I do is for love of you, both this and that." When any contradiction comes upon you, thoroughly resign yourself unto our Lord, and console yourself (De Sales, *Thy Will Be Done*, 12-13).

Prayer: Gentle Jesus, thank you for rising from the dead and assuring me the hope of my own resurrection. Guide me to walk with you, trusting in your promise of rising with you to new life.

Sundays in the Lenten Season

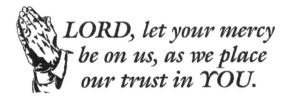

LORD, let your mercy be on us, as we place our trust in YOU.

First Sunday of Lent A

Gen 2: 7-9; 3: 1-7; Ps 51; Rm 5: 12-19; Mt 4: 1-11

Preparation: Take a few minutes of silence, setting aside all your worries and anxieties, and become aware of the divine presence.

Listening to God's Word: Then Jesus was led by the Spirit into the desert to be tempted by the devil. He fasted for forty days and forty nights, and afterwards he was hungry. The tempter approached and said to him, "If you are the Son of God, command that these stones become loaves of bread" (Mt 4: 1-3).

Temptation Against Loyalty

The Sage in the book of Sirach says, "My son, when you come to serve the Lord, prepare yourself for trials. Be sincere of heart and steadfast, undisturbed in time of adversity. Cling to him, forsake him not" (Sir 2: 1-3). This is true of Jesus and all those who follow Him. While reading today's Gospel narrative from the view point of the evangelist, we will understand that the motive of the temptation account is to show the loyalty of Jesus as the true and faithful Son of the Father. In His commitment to fulfill the Father's salvific mission, Jesus faced fierce temptations and struggles. The devil said, "If you are the Son of God, change these stones into bread; if you are the Son of God, jump down from the temple; if you are the Son of God, prostrate and worship me" (cf. Mt 4: 3, 6, 8-9). These were great challenges to His faithfulness and identity as the Son of God. Yet, Jesus remained faithful and steadfast in such difficult times. Jesus' experience of temptation reminds us of the temptation struggle of our first parents, Adam and Eve, who had everything in plenty as they needed, yet yielded to the temptation. What was actually their temptation? To be equal with God, because they were not satisfied with what God had given them. So they aspired to be like God (cf. Gen 3: 5), and instead of showing loyalty they yielded to the temptation of unfaithfulness.

The people of Israel experienced God's marvelous intervention in liberating them from the land of slavery to the land of prosperity and freedom.

They experienced God's protection and guidance in their faith journey. Yet, they had given in to the temptation of unbelief and lack of trust in God, desiring to return back to Egypt (cf. Deut 6: 13). While our first parents and Israel failed in their faithfulness to God, Jesus whom the Father acknowledged at His baptism as "the beloved Son" proved His identity as the faithful Son by overcoming the temptations. Jesus by His temptation experience teaches us today that only by trusting in the power of God we will be able to battle our faults and overcome temptations. Moreover, the temptations of Jesus remind us of our own moments of struggles, trials, and challenges which are the temptations of our daily life. They may come in the form of slothfulness, avarice, and vain ambitions, the excessive desire to fulfill our physical and material needs, and disregarding the needs of others so as to be the biggest and the best of all. How do we face such moments of temptations that occur easily and frequently? As disciples of Jesus, we also need to make sure that we do not cause temptations for others. Jesus' victory over His struggles, suffering, and death dramatizes the lifestyle of the believers by creating them as a community of hope. In the face of temptations, do I believe in God's power or turn against Him? Do I cause temptations for others by my words and actions?

Wisdom from St. Francis de Sales: As long as you feel yourself tempted, follow what little children do when they see a wolf or a bear in the field. They run at once to their father's or mother's arms or at least call out to them for help and assistance. In the same way, have recourse to God, imploring his mercy and his help. If you find, however, that the temptation persists or even grows stronger hasten in spirit to embrace the holy Cross as if you see Jesus Christ crucified before you. Affirm that you will never yield to the temptation and ask him for help against it (De Sales, *IDL, Part IV,* Ch. 7, 307-308).

Prayer: Loving Jesus, thank you for your fidelity to the Father by overcoming the temptations. Guide me in my faith journey to avoid the near occasions to sin and remain faithful to you.

First Sunday of Lent B

Gen 9: 8-15; Ps 25: 4-9; 1Pet 3: 18-22; Mk 1: 12-15

Preparation: Take a few minutes of silence, setting aside all your worries and anxieties, and become aware of the divine presence.

Listening to God's Word: At once the Spirit drove him out into the desert, and he remained in the desert for forty days, tempted by Satan. After John had been arrested, Jesus came to Galilee proclaiming the gospel of God: "This is the time of fulfillment. The kingdom of God is at hand. Repent, and believe in the gospel" (Mk 1: 12, 14-15).

Good News of Hope for New Life

Every day we hear news about destruction, conflict and social turmoil, breakup of marriages and friendships, violence and death, fighting between different groups, and religious tension. All such life realities lead us to believe that our world is a chaotic world. But the Liturgy of the Word at the outset of the holy season of Lent brings us the message of hope that Jesus offers through His victory over the powers of chaos. The temptation of Jesus is clearly linked with His baptism at the Jordan where He experienced the divine world through the empowerment of the Holy Spirit and affirmation by the Father. The same Spirit has led Jesus now into the wilderness which is a symbol of a demonic world of chaos. There He battled with Satan and the powers of evil. It explains that the one who experiences God most profoundly also would face evil with the same intensity. The struggle in the desert is the beginning of Jesus' messianic activity to contain the powers of chaos. This confrontation with the evil powers by Jesus has a messianic element and cosmic dimension. The Holy Spirit, who created order in the world from chaos in the beginning, continues to confront through Jesus the evil powers of cosmic chaos and emerges victorious from this conflict. Hence, the kingdom that Jesus announces is God's reign that overpowers the forces of evil in the world. It is a kingdom that gives us the hope of new life. It is a kingdom that restores everything to its original order of grace. This theme is well explained in God's covenant with Noah (cf. Gen 9: 9-11). The great flood is the symbol of chaos that causes despair, disillusion, and destruction among God's people. But God through His covenant assures that He does not abandon His people.

This is the nature of the kingdom that Jesus proclaimed. So He invites us, "Repent and believe in the Gospel" (Mk 1: 15). In the biblical understanding, "faith in God" generally means not simply intellectual conviction, but "trust, loyalty, and personal commitment" (cf. Gen 15: 6; Ex 4: 4-5; Is 28: 16). Abraham's faith commitment is proven in his loyalty to follow the way of the Lord. His experience tells us that becoming God's people demands commitment to the covenantal relationship with God. In this light, repentance in the preaching of Jesus implies radical change and reorientation for a new existence. Hence, to accept God's kingdom and experience His steadfast love demands faithfulness and change of attitudes toward life. If Jesus the Son of God encountered evil powers, we too would be confronted by the same forces of chaos in our life that might come as sickness, starvation, isolation, failures, and frustration. In such moments we are not lost because our God is not a God of destruction but of salvation. St. Augustine says, "Our pilgrimage is not exempt from trials. We progress by means of trials. If in Christ and for Christ we are tempted, in Christ and through Christ we overcome the devil and the powers of evil." The victory of Jesus over Satan gives us the hope that He empowers us in our weakness and miseries to overcome the chaos in our life (cf. 1Pet 3: 18). What plan of action do I take to reform my life this Lent? What do I see in my life and in the lives of others as Good News of hope?

Wisdom from St. Francis de Sales: It is true, we have to resist great temptations with invincible courage. But perhaps we may be able to gain greater profit resisting well small temptations. Just as the great temptations surpass the small in quality, so the small surpass the great very much in number. In short, little temptations to anger, suspicion, jealousy, envy, flirtations, vanity, frivolity, duplicity, affectation, deceit, unchaste thoughts—these are the trials which even the most devout and resolute must constantly face. Therefore, Philothea, we have to prepare ourselves for this battle with great care and diligence (De Sales, *IDL, Part IV,* Ch. 8, 309-310).

Prayer: Dear Jesus, thank you for the message of hope you offer by defeating the powers of chaos. Help me to be optimistic and courageous in facing the moments of trials in my life.

First Sunday of Lent C

Deut 26: 4-10; Ps 91: 1-2, 10-15; Rm 10: 8-10; Lk 4: 1-13

Preparation: Take a few minutes of silence, setting aside all your worries and anxieties, and become aware of the divine presence.

Listening to God's Word: Filled with the Holy Spirit, Jesus returned from the Jordan and was led by the Spirit into the desert for forty days to be tempted by the devil. He ate nothing during those days, and when they were over he was hungry. The devil said to him, "If you are the Son of God, command this stone to become bread" (Lk 4: 1-2).

Our New Exodus

We normally understand the imagery of wilderness as a place of lifelessness, loneliness, abandonment, and the abode of evil spirits that create a sense of fear and horror. But there is also a Christian perspective of understanding the significance of wilderness as a place of spiritual discernment and growth. In this perspective, Exodus does not mean an experience of struggles, sufferings, and punishment alone. It is a pilgrim journey toward spiritual maturity and experience of God. This is the central message of today's Liturgy of the Word. Exodus for Israel was their religious epic of faith-experience. Their departure from Egypt was a night watching by the Lord to bring them out of the land of slavery (cf. Ex 12: 42). Yahweh led the people from bondage through the wilderness into the promised land of freedom and prosperity (cf. Ex 13: 18). Therefore, the people of Israel kept nostalgic memories of their Exodus journey in the wilderness as their spiritual formation to be God's people. During their journey in the wilderness (cf. Deut 26: 6-9), they experienced the providence of God who protected them from dangers (cf. Ex 14: 30), quenched their thirst, and satisfied their hunger. So they proclaimed with gratitude that God loved and kept them as the apple of His eye; like an eagle, He bore them up on His pinions (cf. Deut 32: 10-11). Thus, the Exodus of Israel was their journey of renewal and recreation as a people belonging to God.

Similarly, the experience of Jesus in the wilderness was His exodus which culminated in His death and resurrection. After His baptism, the Spirit led Jesus into the wilderness not to suffer misfortunes but to gain spiritual discernment and empowerment to make a free decision about His mission. He met in the wilderness angels and devils, and experienced temptations and frustrations. Yet, it was there He proved His identity as "Son of God" and attained spiritual discernment to follow the Father's will. Though Jesus faced the forces of evil throughout His life, He had learned in those moments to depend on the Father guided by the Holy Spirit as His motivating force. In the same way, our life of faith stormed by daily challenges and problems is our new exodus. As believers, we would face evil attractions and allurements, and the destructive powers of bitterness and hatred against people. This is our wilderness experience accompanied by ongoing trials. However, wilderness does not mean the absence of people but the presence of God. Jesus with his exodus-experience is our model and inspiration in our new exodus. If we can see God's hand guiding us in all such moments, we can experience the angels (God's power) guiding us. As the Prophet Isaiah says, in a strange transformation of recreation, we will soon see the desert blossom and the barren lands watered by fertile rivers (cf. Is 41: 16). In my new exodus journey of faith, do I depend on God and prove my identity as a faithful disciple of Jesus? Do I remain optimistic or pessimistic in facing hardships and problems in life?

Wisdom from St. Francis de Sales: So have courage, Philothea, in the midst of temptations. Never think yourself vanquished as long as they are displeasing to you. Note well that there is a difference between feeling and consenting. We may still feel them even though they displease us. However, we cannot consent to them unless we take pleasure in them, because pleasure ordinarily serves as a step to consent. Let the enemies of our salvation set before us their snares and allurements as much as they like. Let them remain always at the door of our heart, seeking entrance. But as long as we are determined to take no pleasure in all this, we can never offend God (De Sales, *IDL, Part IV,* Ch. 3, 300).

Prayer: Lord Jesus, thank you for your discernment to follow the Father's will for my redemption. Help me to see the Father's hand guiding me in my exodus journey of faith.

Second Sunday of Lent A

Gen 12: 1-4; Ps 33; 2Tim 1: 8-10; Mt 17: 1-9

Preparation: Take a few minutes of silence, setting aside all your worries and anxieties, and become aware of the divine presence.

Listening to God's Word: After six days Jesus took Peter, James, and John his brother, and led them up a high mountain by themselves. And he was transfigured before them; his face shone like the sun and his clothes became white as light (Mt 17: 1-2).

Glorification through Crucifixion

The transfiguration experience of Jesus explains His journey to glorification through crucifixion. Jesus as the Son of God (cf. Mt 17: 6), before experiencing glorification, has to be the Son of Man, experiencing suffering and death. Our human experience shows that the successful are those who have struggled in life. Charlie Chaplin, the great comedy actor, was a world famous figure. Many know about his extraordinary talent for making others happy, but only a few might know about the struggles he faced behind his successful life. When he was very young, his mother died of a serious physical illness. He suffered utter poverty and hunger. Life in his family was a continual struggle. To overcome the challenge of survival, Charlie Chaplin at the age of five joined his elder brother to perform street plays and helped to earn an income for the family. His efforts to develop the art of acting began at this very young age, and his continued hard work made him the best comic actor in the world. He even produced a film in 1940, *The Great Dictator,* teasing Hitler, who at the time of its release was the dictator of Germany. The man who experienced poverty, hunger, and the struggles of life, became successful at making people of many generations happy and joyful even in hard times. He reached success through struggles, joy through sufferings, and enjoyment through discouragements. We heard in the first reading about Abraham's faith journey of believing in God's promise at all times. When God called Abraham to leave everything and follow Him, it was a difficult demand. The place was unknown, the road was unclear, the people were unfamiliar, and his safety was uncertain. In fact, Abraham struggled to make the decision whether or not to obey God's command. However, he finally decided to follow the way of God.

As he trusted in God's promise during those difficult moments, God abundantly blessed Abraham to be the father of a great nation and a blessing for others (cf. Gen 12: 2-4). The transfiguration of Jesus, too, explains that His whole life was a journey from His homeland of Nazareth to the land of Calvary, from struggle to success, from humiliation to exaltation, from crucifixion to glorification, from being the Son of Man to also being the faithful Son of God. Though Jesus experienced divine glory as the Son of God (cf. Mt 17: 6), realizing the mission of human redemption to be accomplished, He came down from the mountain of glory to face the realities of life as the Son of Man. Consequently, He won salvation for the world through His death and resurrection (cf. Mt 17: 9). In our life experience, it is natural that we become frustrated in times of failures, disappointed when facing difficulties, and lose hope during struggles. The faith experiences of Abraham and Jesus show that our life must be a journey of faith in the promise of the Lord who would lead us from pain to gain, struggle to success, gloom to happiness, crucifixion to glorification. Clinging on to material comforts and social or ecclesial privileges and positions will make us unworthy instruments to proclaim the message of Jesus who gave up all His prerogatives in order to give us life. How do I face the problems of daily life? Do I cling on to the glorious moments in life, or do I cling on to God in all situations and journey forward with optimism?

Wisdom from St. Francis de Sales: In order to journey steadily, we must apply ourselves to doing well the stretch of road immediately before us on the first day of the journey, and not waste time wanting to do the last lap of the way while we still have to make it through the first. Remember this well: we are sometimes so busy being good angels that we neglect to be good men and women. Our imperfections are going to accompany us to the grave. We can't go anywhere without having our feet on the ground; yet if we fall, we don't just lie there, sprawled in the dust. Our imperfections force us to acknowledge our misery, give us practice in humility, selflessness, patience, and watchfulness; God looks at the preparation of our heart and sees that it is perfect (Thibert, *Golden Counsels of SFS,* 13-14).

Prayer: Loving Jesus, thank you for teaching me to see blessings even in suffering. Guide me in my faith life to rely on your grace and cling on to you even in difficult times.

Second Sunday of Lent B

Gen 22: 1-2, 9-13, 15-18; Ps 118: 10, 15-19;
Rm 8: 31-34; Mk 9: 2-10

Preparation: Take a few minutes of silence, setting aside all your worries and anxieties, and become aware of the divine presence.

Listening to God's Word: He hardly knew what to say, they were so terrified. Then a cloud came, casting a shadow over them; then from the cloud came a voice, "This is my beloved Son. Listen to him." Suddenly, looking around, they no longer saw anyone but Jesus alone with them (Mk 9: 6-8).

Listening to the Lord

Once, a disciple, to express his highest honor and respect to his spiritual master, praised him proudly. So the master humbly said to the disciple, "Light is reflected on the wall. Why venerate the wall? Just be attentive to the light and you will know the truth and understand the reality." Worship that does not effect inner transformation is not worship at all. We can find in Jesus' experience of transfiguration a glimpse of His true identity and the glorious goal to which His journey would lead. St. Paul explains very clearly this identity and the mission of Jesus. He says, "It is Christ Jesus, who died, who was raised, who is at the right hand of God, who indeed intercedes for us" (cf. Rom 8: 34). Jesus loves us so much that He shares with us His own glory with the Father in order that we might be transformed by Him. Hence, transfiguration simply means transformation of the heart. Consequently, we become a "new creation" with positive conviction and a new perspective in life. This radical transformation of the heart implies listening to Jesus. The heavenly voice said, "This is my beloved Son, listen to him" (Mk 9: 7). Jesus throughout His life as God's beloved Son listened and obeyed God's plan and thereby understood the meaning of His suffering and death.

Abraham too listened to God and understood the meaning of his faith and trust, even in the midst of struggles. God's demand for his only son Isaac as a sacrifice was a terrible blow for Abraham. As a human father, he must have struggled in his faith response to meet such a demand from God whom he loved dearly and trusted profoundly. But he approached the problem in a new way. Since he was transformed by his faith experience and listened to God in every event of his life, he was able to respond to God's demand in complete trust. So he experienced great blessings from God, having descendants as numerous as the stars of the sky and as the sand of the sea shore (cf. Gen 22: 17). Thus, Abraham proved his wholehearted commitment to God despite his daily problems and difficulties, struggles, and troubles of life, and emerged as a paragon of faith and trust. As believers, we are to be like Abraham and Jesus listening to God with wholehearted trust in all moments of life. Our faith experience should not be just the following of some religious rituals. It demands a life of surrender as a testimony of God's love. It deals with the affirmation of life with a new perspective in the face of possible difficulties and challenges. Then, transformed by the Lord's grace we will be able to say like St. Paul, "When God is with us, who can be against us" (Rm 8: 31). By attentively listening to God and others with trust, we can find solutions for our many problems, broken relationships can be restored, and those who are depressed and frustrated can be encouraged to find a new direction in life. This Lent invites us to listen to the Lord that we too would emerge as paragons of faith and hope. Do I listen to God speaking to me through others and through life events? Do I listen to people's views and opinions and be attentive to their needs?

Wisdom from St. Francis de Sales: The indifferent heart is like a ball of wax in God's hands, ready to receive all the impressions of His eternal good pleasure. It is a heart without choice, equally ready for all things and having no other object for its will except the will of God. It does not place its love in the things God wills, but in the will of God who wills them. Therefore, when God's will is found in many things, the indifferent heart chooses, no matter what the coast may be, that in which more of God's will abides (De Sales, *Finding God's Will for You*, 84-85).

Prayer: Compassionate Jesus, thank you for your words of inspiration and encouragement. Motivate me with your grace to listen to your words so that I may listen to people in need.

Second Sunday of Lent C

Gen 15: 5-12, 17-18; Ps 27: 1, 7-9, 13-14;
Phil 3: 17-4:1; Lk 9: 28-36

Preparation: Take a few minutes of silence, setting aside all your worries and anxieties, and become aware of the divine presence.

Listening to God's Word: And behold, two men were conversing with him, Moses and Elijah, who appeared in glory and spoke of his exodus that he was going to accomplish in Jerusalem. Peter and his companions had been overcome by sleep, but becoming fully awake, they saw his glory and the two men standing with him (Lk 9: 30-32).

Life-transforming Promise

Hope-giving and life-assuring promises are essential for human progress and growth. Husbands and wives find happiness in their promise of fidelity. Friendships grow stronger by the promise of faithfulness. Children depend very much on the promises of their parents. Students choose subjects that are career promising. Similarly, Abraham in his faith journey took a leap of faith into the hands of God in his faith journey by believing in God's promise of a son and a great nation. But all that he experienced were struggles and trials—no homeland, no children, and no security (cf. Gen 15: 2-3). There was not even a sign of the fulfillment of God's promise. Yet, God did not give up on Abraham. He countered him with a covenant that promised not only a son but numerous progeny like the stars in the sky (cf. Gen 15: 5). Hence, Abraham responded to God's life-assuring promise with deep faith. He believed in all that God said and learned to rely on Him in everything no matter what. This is the promise of Jesus' transfiguration—glory which is permanent and everlasting. But it involves His departure through suffering and death that is momentary and transitory. When the disciples witnessed His dazzling glory, they were awestruck and wanted to capture that consoling moment and linger on the mountain top. So Peter in great enthusiasm said, "Master, it is good that we are here; let us make three tents" (Lk 9: 33). The disciples tried to take refuge in the tents permanently, whereas Jesus guided them to come down from the mountain top and face life in the world with all its adventures and challenges, and thus continue their faith journey toward the resurrection-glory.

As believers in Jesus, we are not to take shelter in what is temporary or transitory but strive to reach our home in heaven steadfastly following the way of Jesus. Unfortunately, the success of human efforts, our free decisions and choices in life that contrast with moral and faith values, and the comforts and luxuries of this world seem to be very promising, assuring us lasting contentment and happiness. We often take refuge in such promises believing that they would give us permanent relief from our problems and troubles. Paradoxically, we soon find ourselves groping in the darkness of dissatisfaction and unhappiness. So St. Paul exhorts us to realize that "our citizenship is in heaven" (Phil 3: 20). Through baptism, we have become God's children and we are called to journey toward our eternal home to share God's glory in Christ. As God's promise sustains our hope of eternal life, we must make a departure from everything that prevents us from living in full communion and right relationship with God and one another. This must be our leap of faith into the hands of God, believing in His promise. If we allow Jesus' words to transform us, transfigure us, and mold us to listen to Him and walk with Him even to Calvary, we will experience the fulfillment of His promise of new life. In my faith life, do I throw myself into the hands of God believing in His life-giving promise, or do I tend to take refuge in the pleasures and luxuries of this world? Are my words and actions life-promising for others?

Wisdom from St. Francis de Sales: On entering God's service many lay down conditions. Is it not clear to you that you are not entrusting your spirit into God's hands as our Lord did? Certainly, it is in this that all our ills, our troubles, our disquietudes and other such nonsense originate. As soon as things do not happen as we had expected or as we had promised ourselves, desolation seizes us. We are not yet perfectly indifferent, totally surrendered into the divine hands (Visitation, *The Sermons of SFS for Lent,* 206).

Prayer: Dear Jesus, thank you for your promise of new life to all who believe in you. Grant me your grace to walk with you by believing in your life-giving promise and never give up.

Third Sunday of Lent A

Ex 17:3-7; Ps 95: 1-2, 6-9; Rm 5: 1-2, 5-8; Jn 4: 5-42

Preparation: Take a few minutes of silence, setting aside all your worries and anxieties, and become aware of the divine presence.

Listening to God's Word: A woman of Samaria came to draw water. Jesus said to her, "Give me a drink." His disciples had gone into the town to buy food. The Samaritan woman said to him, "How can you, a Jew, ask me, a Samaritan woman, for a drink?" (Jn 4: 7-9).

Thirsting for the Living Water

Our present day culture can be described as a pop culture. When people feel thirsty, they do not like to drink water but they immediately look for pop drinks like Coca-Cola, Pepsi, Sprite, or some other drinks. These things may be tasty but do not quench our thirst. We will be thirsty again. Only those who live in draught affected countries will know the true meaning of thirsting for water. The Liturgy of the Word today assures us that Jesus is our living water and if we drink of this water we will never thirst again. Historically, the Samaritans and the pious Jews never had a good relationship because the Samaritans diluted their bloodline by intermarriage and had customs mixed with pagan practices because of the Assyrian invasion. So the southern Jews despised the Samaritans and avoided personal and social relationships with them. In this context, Jesus' encounter with the Samaritan woman was an extremely important face of his mission. There are two movements in this story, namely, God's movement toward His people by thirsting for them, and in turn, people's movement toward God through their inner longing. This is seen clearly in the conversation between Jesus and the Samaritan woman. Jesus as the living water guided the Samaritan woman progressively from ignorance to enlightenment, from doubt to clearer understanding of truth, from brokenness to wholeness, from sinfulness to holiness.

Jesus' request to the woman, "Give me a drink" (Jn 4: 7), shows His thirst for people and His gesture of human solidarity with the despised people, transcending societal and religious differences. Jesus says, "Whoever drinks the water I shall give will never thirst" (Jn 4: 14). What does this water mean? It refers to the revelation of God's love for the world manifested through Jesus who offers eternal life to all who believe in Him. The woman also expressed her inner longing for God, and so she asked Jesus, "Sir, give me that water, so that I may not be thirsty" (v. 15a). Because of this thirst for God, she experienced God's love revealed in Jesus who quenched her longing for freedom, forgiveness, and enlightenment. In the encounter, she experienced new light in her life that was darkened by her own sins and by rejection from society. Consequently, she became the Lord's messenger by sharing the experience with her people. They all came and believed in Him (cf. v. 29). Here God's message of salvation made a great transition, breaking all barriers. On the contrary, the people of Israel (cf. Ex 17: 4-7), after having experienced God's mighty power, began to complain and grumble against God in times of hardship. They even questioned God's life-giving presence by asking, "Is the Lord in our midst or not?" (Ex 17: 7). Through His death and resurrection, Jesus reconciled us with God and one another, transforming us as a new creation. In this way Jesus is "the living water," refreshing us to think and act in a new way, inspiring us to make right decisions, strengthening us in our weakness, and forgiving us when we are in sin. How does Jesus become living water for me in moments of trials, hardships, and problems? Do I feel my thirst and hunger satisfied by coming to Jesus?

Wisdom from St. Francis de Sales: It is very true that in order to surrender ourselves unreservedly to divine providence, we ourselves need to be very trusting. But it is also true that when we let go of everything, our Lord takes care of all and manages all. If we hold back anything—this shows a lack of trust in him—he lets us keep it. It is as if he said, "You think yourself wise enough to handle this matter without me; I allow you to do so; you will see how you come out in the end" (Thibert, *Golden Counsels of SFS,* 20).

Prayer: Loving and caring Jesus, thank you for becoming living water for me. Guide me with your Spirit to thirst for you in all moments that I will learn to approach my life in a new way.

Third Sunday of Lent B

Ex 20: 1-17; Ps 19: 8-11; 1Cor 1: 22-25; Jn 2: 13-25

Preparation: Take a few minutes of silence, setting aside all your worries and anxieties, and become aware of the divine presence.

Listening to God's Word: Since the Passover of the Jews was near, Jesus went up to Jerusalem. He found in the temple area those who sold oxen, sheep, and doves, as well as the money-changers seated there. He made a whip out of cords and drove them all out of the temple area (Jn 2: 13-15).

Zeal for the Lord

Like other religious groups, the people of Israel considered the Ten Commandments and the Temple as the soul of their religious experience. The Ten Commandments were the guiding principles in their fundamental religious orientation as God's chosen people. These divine commandments reflect their identity and add meaning to their life as God's special possession. So God said, "If you hearken to my voice and keep my covenant, you shall be my special possession" (Ex 19: 5). The Temple too had a central place in the life of Israel since it was a symbol of God's living presence among them and a sign of their unity as a worshiping community. Their life guided by the Ten Commandments and the experience of God's presence in the Temple fostered in them a sense of "zeal for the Lord." The term "zeal" in religious experience would mean longing for the Lord, belonging to the Lord, and passionate love for the Lord. With such a passionate love for the Lord the people could understand the real meaning of God's covenant affirmation, "I am your God; you are my people." In this light, the Gospel account of cleansing the Temple by Jesus (cf. Jn 2: 13-16) shows that the real notion of the Temple as God's living presence was lost. The zeal for the Lord was substituted with the external religiosity of the people. Their faithfulness to the covenant relationship with God disappeared. This paradox can be seen in the way worship was organized in the Temple: "Jesus found in the Temple area those who sold oxen, sheep, and doves as well as money changers seated there" (Jn 2: 14).

According to the ancient custom, the religious administrators in the Temple took pains to provide the worshipers a high quality of things for sacrifice. The "dirty" Roman money people brought in could be exchanged for the "holy" Temple money (cf. Jn 2: 14b), and the things sold in the Temple were costlier than things sold outside. Thus, before entering into relationship with God, people had to go through the exploiting system of trade and money exchange. In the house of God, offertory things and Temple money had replaced the God who loves and liberates the people. Thus, God's house of divine presence was turned into a marketplace. So He said, "Stop making my Father's house a marketplace" (Jn 2: 16). The passionate love of Jesus for the Father led Him to being consumed into His Passion and death (vv. 19, 21). But the crucified Jesus continues to reveal the Father's living presence to the believers, leading them to deepen their relationship with Him and live a life of faithfulness to His covenantal love. Karl Rahner said, "The main reason for atheism in the world is Christians themselves. Those who preach God with their words deny him with their lifestyle and that is what the unbelieving world finds simply unbelievable." Therefore, believing in Jesus means doing everything in life out of passionate love for the Lord. This inner longing to live by God's love will lead us to experience the power and the wisdom of Christ crucified (cf. 1Cor 1: 23-25). How do I express my zeal for the Lord—by a life of loyalty or merely expressing my religiosity? Do I show passionate love and caring for the needs of people around me?

Wisdom from St. Francis de Sales: Let us come to his last word: "Father, into your hands I entrust my spirit" (Lk 23:46). This word contains all Christian perfection. In this word is found our Lord's perfect abandonment into His heavenly Father's hands, without any reserve whatever. "I entrust my spirit into your hands." Note here His humility, His obedience, and His true submission. Here is the quintessence of the spiritual life—this perfect abandonment into the hands of the heavenly Father and this perfect indifference in whatever is His divine will (Visitation, *The Sermons of SFS for Lent*, 204-205).

Prayer: Loving Jesus, thank you for expressing your passionate love for me by your death. Help me to learn from you to show my deep love for you and my brothers and sisters in truthfulness.

Third Sunday of Lent C

Ex 3: 1-8a, 13-15; Ps 103: 1-4, 6-8, 11;
1Cor 10: 1-6, 10-12; Lk 13: 1-9

Preparation: Take a few minutes of silence, setting aside all your worries and anxieties, and become aware of the divine presence.

Listening to God's Word: "He said to the gardener, 'For three years now I have come in search of fruit on this fig tree but have found none. So cut it down. Why should it exhaust the soil?' He said to him in reply, 'Sir, leave it for this year also, and I shall cultivate the ground around it and fertilize it; it may bear fruit in the future. If not, you can cut it down'" (Lk 13: 7-9).

The Extended Time of Grace

Today's Liturgy of the Word illustrates the extended time of God's grace that demands renewal and a life of fruitfulness. The image of the fruitless fig tree is a beautiful parable illustrating the nature of God's mercy and our response of faithfulness. The owner of the land waited three years (cf. Lk 13: 6) expecting fruits from the fig tree. It is a long period of time that the owner waited patiently but in vain. The situation turned out to be fruitless and hopeless. So it was the right time to cut down the tree (cf. Lk 13: 8). However, the gardener pleaded for giving the tree yet another chance. This is a beautiful illustration to explain the extended time of grace from God who is a God of life and love. As such, He waits patiently and passionately for our renewal. Fullness of life means living with others and for others and this is what God does for us as He is merciful, loving, and compassionate. This is seen in His initiative to liberate Israel from their slavery. God said to Moses, "I have witnessed the affliction of my people and have heard their cry of complaint. Therefore, I have come down to rescue them" (Ex 3: 7-8). Such is our God who is the God of compassion and not of punishment. He is not interested in the death of sinners but in their redemption. So He says, "I take no pleasure in the death of the wicked man, but rather in the wicked man's conversion that he may live. Turn, turn from your evil ways! Why should you die?" (Ez 33: 11).

God's purpose of His extended time of grace for us is to live as renewed people bearing fruits of faithfulness. This parable also describes what is sin. It is an unproductive life and a lack of loving communion with God and others. Jesus says, "If you do not repent, you will all perish as they did" (Lk 13: 5). It evokes in us the realization that the unexpected crisis moment of the end time will come for one whether righteous or unrighteous. As all sin, so all will die but as the invitation of grace offered by Jesus is free and unearned, faithful response of fruitfulness is expected at the time of reckoning. The gratuitous extension of the time of grace is not unlimited time. We cannot take God's patience and mercy for granted and procrastinate in wasting our time and talents. So what must we do? We are called to repent and renew our life and come back to the Lord, growing in loving communion. God's gracious gifts and opportunities are intended to bring transformation of the heart and renewal in life. This was the warning of St. Paul to the Corinthian community not to be overconfident of the privileges but to learn from the experiences of Israel in the wilderness to be watchful (cf. 1Cor 10: 6, 10-11), renewing their Christian commitments in following Jesus. This season of Lent is the extended time of grace given to us. Do I recognize in gratitude God's graciousness and mercy? Do I make use of the extended time of grace as another opportunity to repent from my evil ways and bear fruits of faithfulness? Have I taken the Lord's call to renewal seriously?

Wisdom from St. Francis de Sales: God loves with intensely tender love those of us who are happy enough to abandon ourselves entirely to his fatherly care, letting ourselves be governed by his divine providence without wasting time by considering if the effects of this providence will be useful, profitable, or harmful for us. We can be assured that from all that has been sent to us from his fatherly and lovable heart, God will draw goodness and value, provided that we have placed all our confidence in him and that we say willingly, "I place my spirit—my soul, my body, and all that I am—into your blessed hands" to do with me as you wish (Thibert, *Golden Counsels of SFS,* 18).

Prayer: Dear Jesus, thank you for the many opportunities of blessings in my life. Guide me to be grateful to you and use every opportunity as your extended time of grace for renewal of my life.

Fourth Sunday of Lent A

1Sam 16: 1, 6-7, 10-13; Ps 23: 1- 6; Eph 5: 8-14; Jn 9: 1-41

Preparation: Take a few minutes of silence, setting aside all your worries and anxieties, and become aware of the divine presence.

Listening to God's Word: When Jesus heard that they had thrown him out, he found him and said, "Do you believe in the Son of Man?" He answered and said, "Who is he, sir, that I may believe in him?" Jesus said to him, "You have seen him and the one speaking with you is he." He said, "I do believe, Lord," and he worshiped him (Jn 9: 35-38).

Coming to the Light

Once, a disciple asked the spiritual teacher, "Why is it that everyone here is happy and joyful except me?" "Because they have learned to see goodness and beauty everywhere," the master said. "Why don't I see the same goodness and beauty everywhere?" asked the disciple. "Because you cannot see outside of you what you fail to see inside of you," the teacher replied. The Liturgy of the Word today inspires us to come to Jesus the light in order to see goodness, beauty, and happiness around us. The Gospel narrative is a beautiful illustration of believers' progressive journey toward light. We find two contrasting movements in the story: the man born blind moves from his physical blindness toward full sight (cf. Jn 9: 1-30), whereas the faith of the religious leaders is marked by blindness of unbelief. The neighbors saw him only as a blind beggar punished by God (v. 8). The leaders could not accept the healing of the blind man and so they accused him of being born in sin (vv. 18, 34). They could not see the goodness of the poor man and the light of divine revelation outside of themselves because they failed to see it within themselves. On the other hand, the blind man through his encounter with Jesus received his physical and spiritual sight and progressed to realize the divine light around him (vv. 11-12), convinced of his faith experience (v. 17), he defended his faith witness (vv. 25-34). It is a wonderful lesson for us in our faith journey. Though the man healed of his blindness could see the goodness of God's beauty around, he had to experience the dark side of life's realities by enduring insult, suspicion, opposition, and accusation of being born in sin.

With his encounter with Jesus, he was restored to wholeness of health and still he was thrown out from society and the community because of his faith witness. They did not accept his testimony of the light (v. 34). This time he accepted the challenges of rejection and opposition with courage and new vision. He was not afraid of anybody or anything. So he said, "If this man were not from God, he would not be able to do anything" (v. 33). His faith explains that to experience joy in life and to face the mounting challenges, we need God's light of right understanding, courage, and determination. Jesus is that light, and we need to come to Him, for He said, "I am the light of the world; whoever follows me will never walk in darkness but will have the light of life" (cf. Jn 8: 12; 9: 5). The man healed of his blindness finding that light followed Jesus by professing, "I do believe, Lord" (9: 38), whereas the religious leaders and the neighbors became blind as they refused to accept the true light. It is our spiritual blindness that creates blind spots in our life. We often wish to prefer darkness to light because it is pleasing to us. St. Paul exhorts us to be aware that we have found the light of life in Christ Jesus and so we are to live as children of light (cf. Eph 5: 8). Jesus as the light heals our blind spots when we come to Him in faith. By following His light, we will be enlightened to see goodness around us, the positive side of things happening to us, and God's presence in every event of life. During this Lent, what do I see around me—goodness or brokenness, light or darkness? Do I lead others to find Jesus the light or lead them into darkness?

Wisdom from St. Francis de Sales: You say, "I am so imperfect." I quite understand you! You should not dream of living in this world without committing some imperfections or the other. What is important is that you should not be attached to your imperfections. You should not commit them deliberately and you should not persevere in committing them. Having said this, now I ask you to remain at peace. Do not fret nor be worried about the perfection to which you aspire with so many ardors. Do not be afraid nor anxious. Walk firmly and confidently. If you are shielded by the armor of faith, nothing on earth will be able to harm you (Tissot, *The Art of Utilizing Our Faults According to SFS,* 54-55).

Prayer: Lord Jesus, thank you for being the light of the world. Lead me with your grace to follow you, the light, with steadfastness that I will be able to see goodness and love in my life.

Fourth Sunday of Lent B

2Chron 36: 14-16, 19-23; Ps 137: 1-6;
Eph 2: 4-10; Jn 3: 14-21

Preparation: Take a few minutes of silence, setting aside all your worries and anxieties, and become aware of the divine presence.

Listening to God's Word: God so loved the world that he gave his only Son, so that everyone who believes in him might not perish but might have eternal life. For God did not send his Son into the world to condemn the world, but that the world might be saved through him (Jn 3: 16-17).

The Divine Character of Love

Once, a beautiful princess on an evening walk through the forest found a frog speaking human language. The frog greeted her and said, "Your royal highness, I am not really a frog. I am a prince but a witch turned me into a frog." The princess in her kindness to help asked the frog-prince, "Is there anything that I can do for you to break this bondage?" The frog replied, "Certainly, you can do something for me. While turning me into a frog, the witch told me that if I could find a princess and stay with her three days and three nights, the spell would be broken and I would be a prince again." The princess, out of love and affection for him, carried the frog to the palace. Seeing this strange behavior of the princess, everyone said, "What a repugnant creature she is carrying around." She kindly replied to them, "No. It is not a repugnant creature. It is a royal prince." And she kept the frog-prince with her for three days and nights. On the third day, she woke up and saw a young, handsome prince who thanked her for breaking the spell of bondage for him. The story of our human life is more or less like the story of the frog. The prince becoming a frog is the creation of our own world according to our personal whims and fancies, a world of sinfulness where we have lost our true identity, the real meaning and the purpose of our life. Yet, there is a hope of new life for us because of the "divine character of love" manifested in Jesus. John says, "God so loved the world that he gave his only Son" (cf. Jn 3: 16). This is indeed God's marvelous way of saving humanity from sin and suffering.

Israel experienced God's compassion that saved them from their Babylonian exile despite their rebellion and hardheartedness (cf. 2Chron 36: 15, 23; Ezra 1: 2-4). The only reason for the divine character of God's love is that He created us in His own image and likeness (cf. Gen 1: 27), has chosen us as His own, and so He loves us beyond our human sinfulness. God, because of His steadfast love, identified Himself with us in our sufferings and wretchedness and gave His only Son in order to lead us to a glorious life. St. Paul tells us, "God, who is rich in mercy, because of the great love he had for us, even when we were dead in our transgressions, brought us to life with Christ…raised us up…and seated us with him" (cf. Eph 2: 4-6). We can notice here the sharp contrast between the greatness of God's steadfast love and our human weakness. This divine character of love is measured by the gift of God's beloved Son: "Everyone who believes in him might not perish but may have eternal life. For God did not send the Son into the world to condemn the world, but that the world might be saved through him" (Jn 3: 16-17). This saving act of Jesus is symbolized in the Son of Man being lifted up (v. 14), which is His death on the Cross and exaltation in resurrection. The fruit of this saving act of God is the "new birth into eternal life" to all who gaze upon the exalted Christ on the Cross in faith. What is my response to this marvelous act of God's love for me? How do I demonstrate in life my love for God?

Wisdom from St. Francis de Sales: The bees have no other remedy for its sickness but to expose itself to the rays of the sun, expecting heat and healing from its splendor. Let us place ourselves before the crucified and say to him, "O splendid sun of our hearts, you will revive us with the rays of your goodness. Here we are almost dead before you; we will not move from here until your heat brings us back to life" (De Sales, *Letters,* 904, from *Every Day with SFS*, 4).

Prayer: Loving Jesus, thank you for revealing to me the divine character of God's love by finding solidarity with me. Help me to live by your love and find fraternal solidarity with others.

Fourth Sunday of Lent C

Joshua 5: 9-12; Ps 34: 2-7; 2Cor 5: 17-21; Lk 15: 1-3, 11-32

Preparation: Take a few minutes of silence, setting aside all your worries and anxieties, and become aware of the divine presence.

Listening to God's Word: So he got up and went back to his father. While he was still a long way off, his father caught sight of him, and was filled with compassion. He ran to his son, embraced him and kissed him. His son said to him, "Father, I have sinned against heaven and against you; I no longer deserve to be called your son" (Lk 15: 20-21).

The Prodigal Father

In a way, the parable of the prodigal son retells the daily experiences of family conflicts between brothers and sisters, parents and children, husband and wife. Though it is traditionally explained as the story of the prodigal son, I invite you to reflect on the role of the prodigal father who suffered enormous mental and psychological pain and agony because of his two sons. According to the social cultural context of the time, the fathers could distribute their property between their children only at the time of their own death (cf. Sir 33: 20-24). When the younger son demanded his share of the family property, he in fact acted shamefully, wishing his father was already dead. Moreover, by selling the property and leaving the family (cf. Lk 15: 13), he failed to honor his father and mother (cf. Ex 20: 12). It was a great insult to the father and a disgrace for the family. Furthermore, while refusing to reconcile with his father and brother as the culture demanded, the behavior of the elder son was also as equally shameful. He publically insulted and humiliated his father by his angry protests, accusations of favoritism, and his bitter alienation (cf. Lk 15: 28-30). However, the outstanding aspect of this parable is the prodigality of the father's love in responding to his sons' humiliating behaviors. In spite of the son's frivolous lifestyle and ruthless behavior, the father was longingly waiting for his return. In fact, it is the father who became prodigal at the loss of his son.

The father's inner longing is expressed in his reaction at the sight of the wayward son's homecoming. "Filled with compassion, he ran to his son, embraced him and kissed him" (v. 20). Here the father acted totally out of cultural character. This was not a dignified behavior expected in the culture from an elderly gentleman. Running, embracing and kissing the wayward son explain that the father's forgiveness was total and complete. The ceremonial family celebration of the son's return means acceptance by the community. The father did not accuse or punish the son for his carelessness and selfishness but took the initiative to recognize and honor him as the true son even before he had a chance to express his repentance. The father was the first one to rejoice at the son's return. He even tried to reconcile the rebellious elder son (cf. vv. 31-32). Thus, the father's even-handed compassion extended equally to both of his sons stands as the emblem of the heavenly Father's love to welcome all people with compassion. God as a loving Father does not punish us for our sinfulness of unfaithfulness to His covenantal love but becomes prodigal because of us, while anxiously longing for our return. He is the first one to rejoice at our homecoming. He forgives us unconditionally, empowers us to begin a fresh start, and recognizes us as dear sons and daughters. St. Paul teaches us that God has reconciled and forgiven us through Christ Jesus while not counting our trespasses (cf. 2Cor 5: 18-20). During this Lent, we must get up resolutely from our brokenness and come to God our Father. Can I come to the Father and say in repentance, "Father I have sinned against you and against my brothers and sisters?" Do I make my father and mother prodigal because of my actions and behaviors?

Wisdom from St. Francis de Sales: Meanwhile, no matter how obstinate sinners may be, we must never lose courage in aiding and serving them. How do we know whether perhaps they will do penance and be saved? As long as we are within the limits of hope that the sinner can amend, and they are always of the same extent as those of his life, we must never reject him, but rather pray for him and help him as far as his misfortune will permit (De Sales, *Finding God's Will for You*, 103-104).

Prayer: Lord Jesus, thank you for revealing the Father's love who is anxiously waiting for my return. Give me the grace to rise up and come back to the Father with repentance and renewal.

Fifth Sunday of Lent Λ

Ez 37: 12-14; Ps 130: 1-8; Rm 8: 8-11; Jn 11: 1-45

Preparation: Take a few minutes of silence, setting aside all your worries and anxieties, and become aware of the divine presence.

Listening to God's Word: Jesus told her, "I am the resurrection and the life; whoever believes in me, even if he dies, will live, and everyone who lives and believes in me will never die. Do you believe this?" She said to him, "Yes, Lord. I have come to believe that you are the Messiah, the Son of God" (Jn 11: 25-27).

The Meaning of Life and Death

Death is an inescapable reality of human life but no one prefers it as everyone loves to live. A disciple once asked his spiritual master, "Is there life after death? If there is one, what would be the nature of such life?" The master replied, "The question is not whether there is life after death, rather the real question is, is there life before death?" Jesus assures eternal life to all those who believe in Him. The dried-up bones given life (cf. Ez 37: 4-6) and the dead Lazarus coming back to life (cf. Jn 11: 43-44) are two images that explain the meaning of life and death for believers. The life of Israel during their exile in Babylon was darkened by miseries and misfortunes, hardships and trials. They struggled physically and spiritually as slaves and refugees losing everything in life. Their life of hopelessness in such a situation was like the dried-up bones, faceless and lifeless. So they cried out, "Our bones are dried up, our hope is lost, and we are cut off" (Ez 37: 11). Ezekiel, as one of the exiled people, preached God's word to bring new life to the dead Israel, "You shall know that I am Lord, when I open your graves and have you rise from them. I will put my spirit in you that you may live" (vv. 13-14). This was in fact a powerful message of hope for the people in exile. The miraculous raising of Lazarus from the dead illustrates God's ultimate power over the course of life and death. The thrust of this whole narrative is that Jesus is the resurrection and the life; everyone who believes in Him will live even in death. "Everyone who lives and believes in Him will not die" (cf. Jn. 11: 25-26).

Hence, to believe in Him as the resurrection means that physical death has no power over believers; their future is determined by their faith in Jesus (cf. 5: 28-29). "Everyone who sees the Son and believes in him may have eternal life" (Jn 6: 40). In the same way, to believe in Jesus as the life means that the believers' present life is also determined by Jesus' power to give eternal life (cf. 3: 16). Moreover, the words of Jesus offer a new vision for believers to understand that life and death belong to the on-going, life-giving power of God in Jesus—even if they die, they will live (cf. 11: 25b), and everyone who lives and believes in Him will live forever (v. 26a). Thus, accepting Jesus as our resurrection and life means believing in the fullness of His relationship with God and in His power to give us life. Our faith in Jesus is fundamentally a total belonging to Him that creates a personal communion with Him and with one another. However, while going through moments of living "death experiences" such as the breakdown of marriages, disappointments, being beaten and pressed down by injustice, and all such evils, people destroy their own life or the lives of others. These are the stones that cover us in our own graves. We feel like the dried-up bones being cut off from our living God. Even in such miserable situations, Jesus assures us the hope of a new beginning. Do I realize that His promise revitalizes my faith and rekindles my hope, removing the stones of death from my life? How do I accept Jesus as the way to new life?

Wisdom from St. Francis de Sales: There are some people who ask our Lord that they might die, and when they are asked why, they answer: "It is to be delivered from the miseries of this life." Others say that they would not fret about dying, provided they were certain of going to Paradise. But even if you were certain of going to Paradise, it would not be appropriate either to desire or to ask for it in order simply to be delivered from the miseries of this world, but only on condition that such be God's will. We must neither desire nor ask for death, nor refuse it when it comes. In this consists the summary of Christian perfection: to ask for nothing and to refuse nothing (Visitation, *The Sermons of SFS for Lent,* 138).

Prayer: Loving Jesus, thank you for your hope-giving promise to make my life and death meaningful. Guide me to find my life worth living, even in the face of "death experiences."

Fifth Sunday of Lent B

Jer 31: 31-34; Ps 51: 3-4, 12-15; Heb 5: 7-9; Jn 12: 20-33

Preparation: Take a few minutes of silence, setting aside all your worries and anxieties, and become aware of the divine presence.

Listening to God's Word: Jesus answered them, "The hour has come for the Son of Man to be glorified. Amen, amen, I say to you, unless a grain of wheat falls to the ground and dies, it remains just a grain of wheat; but if it dies, it produces much fruit. Whoever loves his life loses it, and whoever hates his life in this world will preserve it for eternal life" (Jn 12: 23-25).

Following the Lord in Faithfulness

Once, a young man visited the spiritual master and expressed his desire to be his disciple. To him the master replied, "You may live with me as long as you want but don't become my follower." "Whom, then, should I follow?" the youngster asked. "No one. The day you follow someone you cease to know the truth and follow the truth with conviction," the master replied. Jesus as the Truth says, "Whoever serves me, must follow me" (Jn 12: 26a). This is the message of the Liturgy of the Word: to follow the Lord in faithfulness. The Greeks, after knowing about Jesus' miraculous performances, came to see Him (cf. Jn 12: 21). Here their request "to see" means more than curiosity. It is not a casual visit. It means affirmation of Jesus' teachings and acceptance of Him as the one who reveals God. So their desire to see Jesus meant that they came to believe in Him. But Jesus revealed to them the goal of His mission that involved His personal self-gift. Therefore, He said, "The hour has come for the Son of Man to be glorified" (cf. Jn 12: 23). His hour entails death which is illustrated by the parable of the seed. "If a grain of wheat falls to the ground and dies, it bears much fruit" (cf. v. 24). This image explains the kind of death He suffered in order to give life to the world. The seed of wheat must lose itself to produce a new plant and a bountiful harvest. It signifies a new beginning, new life, and new possibilities. Following Jesus' way always involves sacrifices and giving up personal interests. We can do this because Jesus has done it first Himself. Falling into the ground like a seed and being lifted up on the Cross are images that portray the hour of Jesus' self-gift for the world.

The hour of His glorification was the moment of gathering all people unto Himself in union with the Father (cf. v. 32). This is the mission of Jesus, and all who follow Him must be prepared for this self-gift because the disciples are to be where the master is (cf. v. 26 b). The disciples are to know that to serve the Lord is to look beyond the absolutes of this world and to fall into the ground in loving service of "letting go" of personal concerns. The pact of the new covenant that Jeremiah announced to the people of Israel demonstrates the mutual belongingness and faithfulness between God and people. So the Lord said, "I will place my law within them and write it upon their hearts; I will be their God and they will be my people" (Jer 31: 33). Jesus, affirming our belongingness with God through his death on the Cross, restored us to new life (cf. Heb 5: 9). Hence, believing in Jesus means free and total surrender to Him in love and becoming like seeds to bear much fruit as faithful disciples. Therefore, by following Jesus' example we are to face the hours of our hardships and challenges that might come due to physical illness, problems in our families, and discouragement. Our human tendency to hang on, preserve the status quo, having a no-risks existence, unwillingness to change and welcome new initiatives, not ready to die to self and come out alive for others is not a true life worth living as followers of Jesus. Do I get motivated by the Eucharistic Lord and believe in His promise of new life? Do I show fidelity in following the way of Jesus?

Wisdom from St. Francis de Sales: If you feel that you have been unfaithful to the Lord, here is what you should do, for it is important that you do your best to remain faithful to him. Never be surprised to feel deep within yourself that you are weak, infirm and unfaithful. Remember that God has seen things far worse than these. He is so good and so merciful. He will never cast us out nor abandon us in our wretchedness, but rather give us more grace and do everything possible for our well being and redemption. That is why I say that our miseries are the throne of his mercy (Tissot, *The Art of Utilizing Our Faults According to SFS,* 139-140).

Prayer: Dear Jesus, thank you for leading me to find new life by your death and resurrection. Lead me with your grace to remain faithful in following you and never turn back at any cost.

Fifth Sunday of Lent C

Is 43: 16-21; Ps 126: 1-6; Phil 3: 8-12; Jn 8: 1-11

Preparation: Take a few minutes of silence, setting aside all your worries and anxieties, and become aware of the divine presence.

Listening to God's Word: Then Jesus straightened up and said to her, "Woman, where are they? Has no one condemned you?" She replied, "No one, sir." Then Jesus said, "Neither do I condemn you. Go, and from now on do not sin any more" (Jn 8: 10-11).

No Condemnation but Compassion

Our common human experience shows that forgiveness is, by nature, not only difficult, it is also dangerous and challenging as it would dismantle the systems and customs we have preserved for keeping things under our control. This is explained in the Gospel story about the adulterous woman forgiven by Jesus. A closer reading of the story will tell us of the double-standard of social justice and God's compassion taking the side of disadvantaged people. Only the woman in the story is apprehended, guilty of adultery. What about her partners? While the woman's sin is regarded very serious, the men's sin is regarded less serious. This is the alleged justice in its double-standard. Though the woman standing in shame and humiliation in the midst of those self-righteous men may be guilty of violating marital trust, she was also a marginalized and vulnerable woman in her society. Therefore, she represents all those who are disadvantaged and less privileged, pushed to the margins of society. This serves as the immediate reason to heighten Jesus' kindness and compassion for her. Therefore, He said to the self-righteous group of men, "Let the one among you who is without sin be the first to throw a stone at her" (Jn 8: 7). They went away one by one because they also were guilty of sin and in need of forgiveness.

The motive of the scribes and the Pharisees in bringing the woman to Jesus was not to uphold the Law of Moses but to trap Jesus (cf. Jn 8: 6). They boasted that they caught the woman committing sin and now they also caught Jesus. If Jesus would decide against the death penalty, He would be accused of condoning adultery and disregarding the Mosaic Law. If He agreed to her being stoned to death, He would be accused of blood thirst and denouncing the Romans who had deprived the Jewish authority the power to carry out any death penalty on their own. Here we can notice that while the self-righteous ones chatter about both of them, the Holy One and the sinful one encounter each other. St. Augustine describes this meeting as *misera et misericordia*, that is, misery and mercy meeting, sin and forgiveness facing each other, and condemnation and compassion confronting one another. Without minimizing or justifying her sinfulness, Jesus showed due respect and honor to her as a human person and valued her repentance and conversion more than a just reprisal of her sinfulness. So He showed compassion and mercy by exhorting her, "Neither do I condemn you. Go and from now on do not sin anymore" (v. 11b). By extending unconditional forgiveness to the woman, Jesus erased any false images of an angry God punishing people for their sinfulness and failures. Thus, this story describes that God's loving compassion is extended to all regardless of their social and economic status. So must our love be extended to everyone. During this Lent, let us learn that the life-giving newness of God can be born out of conversion and not coercion, out of compassion and not condemnation. Is it possible to forgive one another and forget? Can I give the last chance of grace to people whom I have cut out of my life? Do I look at the sinfulness of others' past or their goodness of what they could become?

Wisdom from St. Francis de Sales: Even though our Lord cried out again and again, "Blessed are the poor in spirit, the peacemakers, the meek, they who hunger and thirst for justice" (Matt 5:3-6), the world cannot embrace this wisdom. It cries out, "Oh! How blessed are the wealthy, the oppressors, those who take vengeance on their enemies, and those whom one dares not offend." See how the perfection of the Cross is folly in the eyes of the world precisely because it embraces what is abhorrent to human nature. It loves correction and submits to it; it not only takes pleasure in being corrected, but it has no greater pleasure than in being reproved and corrected for faults and failings (Visitation, *The Sermons of SFS for Lent,* 166-167).

Prayer: Loving Jesus, thank you for teaching me the need to be compassionate and forgiving. Guide me with your Spirit to avoid biased judgments and to forgive others generously.

Passion Sunday

Mt 26:14 - 27:66 (A); Mk 14:1 - 15:47 (B); Lk 22:14 - 23:56 (C)

Preparation: Take a few minutes of silence, setting aside all your worries and anxieties, and become aware of the divine presence.

Listening to God's Word: Then going out he went, as was his custom, to the Mount of Olives, and the disciples followed him. When he arrived at the place he said to them, "Pray that you may not undergo the test." After withdrawing about a stone's throw from them and kneeling, he prayed, saying, "Father, if you are willing, take this cup away from; still, not my will but yours be done" (Lk 22: 39-42).

No Turning Back

Pope John Paul II said, "'Passion' means a passionate love, unconditional self-giving: Christ's passion is the summit of an entire life 'given' to his brothers and sisters to reveal the heart of the Father. The Cross, which seems to rise up from the earth, in actual fact reaches down from heaven, enfolding the universe in a divine embrace. The Cross reveals itself to be the centre, meaning and goal of all history and of every human life." This teaching captures the true meaning of Jesus' Passion. He suffered as an innocent victim not to protect his honor and glory but rather to redeem us from sin and restore us to eternal life. In this light, His suffering and death reflect the suffering and struggle of innocent people victimized by violence and injustice in our world. We can notice in the Passion account Jesus' attitude of determination to comply with the Father's plan of human salvation, and not turn back. It is on the Mount of Olives that He began to experience His Passion so intensively. He foresaw the prelude of the kind of suffering that He had to endure, and therefore, He had to make a crucial decision whether to face this battle or to turn back. At this challenging moment, He freely decided to accept with determination the consequences of His mission.

Jesus could see in that moment of prayer, on the one hand, the terrible suffering and agony awaiting Him; on the other hand, the salvation of the world hanging in the balance. He realized that the hour of darkness was deepening (v. 14). The primal acts of abandonment, betrayal, and denial by His own disciples and being treated like a criminal were the moments of darkness that had intensified His agony. At this moment He prayed fervently, "Father, if you are willing, take away this cup from me" (v. 42). This was the strongest expression of Jesus' human anguish to get rid of the cup of suffering. He had the choice for flight or to fight the battle. He could have rejected it. Yet, He decided to be obedient to the Father. The consequence of this decision was the culmination of His self-emptiness for the redemption of the world (cf. Phil 2: 6). In fulfilling His radical decision, Jesus displayed faithfulness to His mission and complete trust in the Father. As disciples of Jesus, we might face our human life with its bright days and dark moments. There may be many gardens of Gethsemane where we may experience denial of human rights and privileges, betrayal of faithfulness and fidelity, situations of failures and frustration, discouragement and dejection. We might feel we are left alone to fight the battle by ourselves. What is our attitude in such moments of darkness? Here, Jesus is our model to stand firm in our decision of "not turning back." We must courageously decide to place the Cross before us and the world behind us and follow Jesus without turning back. What decisions do I make at the time of challenges and hardships? Am I tempted to turn back from my responsibilities and commitments or turn to God in confidence believing that He will defend and guide me?

Wisdom from St. Francis de Sales: Since God's Son was crucified for us, what remains for us at this hour but to crucify with Him our flesh with its passions and desires (2Cor 5:15; Gal 5:24). For love is repaid with love alone. By rendering our Lord love for love and the praises and blessings we owe Him for His death and passion, we will be confessing Him as our liberator and Savior (Visitation, *The Sermons of SFS for Lent*, 186).

Prayer: My Lord, you came not to be served nor to be adored and admired but to have your disciples follow you. Grant us your grace that we may not be caught up with our own man-made belief of admiring you but understand you and follow you in truth and faithfulness (Søren Kierkegaard, Danish philosopher).

Bibliography

De Mello, Anthony. *The Song of the Bird*. New York, NY: Doubleday, 1982.

De Sales, Saint Francis. *Thy Will Be Done: Letters to Persons in the World*. Manchester, NH: Sophia Institute Press, 1995.

_____. *Finding God's Will for You*. Manchester, NH: Sophia Institute Press, 1963.

_____. *Introduction to the Devout Life*. 2nd edition. Bangalore, India: SFS Publications, 1995.

_____. *The Art of Loving God*. Manchester, NH: Sophia Institute Press, 1998.

Klauder, Francis J., ed. *Every Day with St. Francis de Sales*. New Rochelle, NY: Salesiana Publishers, 1985.

Nouwen, Henri M. *From Fear to Love*. Fenton, MO: Creative Communication for the Parish, 1988.

Reid, Barbara E. *Daily Reflections for Lent 2007*. Cincinnati, OH: St. Anthony Messenger Press, 2006.

Sica, Joseph F. *Living with Passion*. New London, CT: Twenty-Third Publications, 2009.

Thibert, Peronne Marie, trans. *Francis de Sales, Jane de Chantal: Letters of Spiritual Direction*. Mahwah, NJ: Paulist Press, 1988.

_____. *Golden Counsels of Saint Francis de Sales*. Monastery of the Visitation, St. Louis, MO, 2006.

Tissot, Joseph, ed. *The Art of Utilizing Our Faults According to St. Francis de Sales*. Bangalore, India: SFS Publications, 1994.

Visitation, Nuns of the, trans. *The Sermons of St. Francis de Sales for Lent.* Rockford, IL: Tan Books and Publishers, Inc., 1987.

Lenten Clip Art. First page of Sundays in the Lenten Season from diocesan publication with permission. All other clip art retrieved from https://www.google.com/search?q=lenten+art+clips&tbm=isch&tbo= u&source=univ&sa=X&ei=Rx51Upe7BIat2AXeyICYBw&ved=0CCw QsAQ&biw=1024&bih=537. Accessed on November 2, 2013.

Gospel Meditations for Lent: Coming Home to the Father contains a beautiful illustration of the core message of the Gospel. The book brings forth the spiritual wisdom of St. Francis de Sales through Scriptural images, stories, life and faith experiences. We must stop leveraging our past mistakes, failures, and sins but start all over again, accepting ourselves as sinners and accepting the forgiving love of the Father. These life-changing and powerful meditations can change the rejected and dejected part of each one of us into the cornerstone of our new and transformed life in Christ. God's mercy is poured out into our hearts through the death and resurrection of Jesus, not because we deserve it but because God loves us.

Rev. Dr. Abraham Vettuvellil, msfs
Superior General of the Missionaries of St. Francis de Sales
Rome, Italy

The new book *Gospel Meditations for Lent* by Fr. Santhiyagu Arockiyasamy, msfs, is full of wisdom. It is the fruit of his study, prayer, and experience as a parish priest both in India and in the United States. Fr. Santhiyagu knows people; he knows the Scriptures, and he knows intimately the spirit of St. Francis de Sales. In this book, the reflection for each day calls the reader to make a quiet and prayerful environment, so the Word of God might be heard. Our salvation and growth is linked in a certain way to the salvation and progress of others around us. This little book is in fact a challenge to let the Word of God penetrate more deeply into our lives: a perfect fit for Lent. I hope you enjoy this book and may the Spirit of Jesus bring us all closer to God.

Rev. Msgr. Michael D. Hazard
Vicar General
Diocese of Kalamazoo, MI

The season of Lent calls us to conversion, repentance, and transformation of our life in Christ. Fr. Santhiyagu Arockiyasamy's reflections on the Scripture readings of Lent provide an opportunity for readers to break open God's word and find new possibilities for furthering their spiritual journey. Readers will find the Gospel wisdom of Jesus and the teachings of St. Francis de Sales come alive in the meditations of this book. May this book be a blessing to all readers and renew the promise of God's unconditional and everlasting Love. May it challenge you to repentance, conversion, and personal transformation during this Lenten season.

Rev. Fr. Augustine Tharappel, msfs
Vice-Provincial of the Missionaries of St. Francis de Sales
USA Vice-Province

Gospel Meditations for Lent: Coming Home to the Father is the fruit of deep reflection by Fr. Santhiyagu Arockiyasamy, msfs, rooted in the Gospel, nurtured by the lived experience of his religious commitments and priestly life for the last seventeen years in witnessing to the Lord. Having experienced the Love of God, the author as path-finder offers to the readers a path to come back to God the Father, who is LOVE and is passionately searching for the lost one: This could be you or me. I appreciate the author for his hard work and recommend this book to all those who seek to return to the Father during this Lent.

Rev. Fr. Anthony Dharmaraj, msfs
Provincial of the Missionaries of St. Francis de Sales
Southeast-India Province

About the Author

Rev. Dr. Santhiyagu Arockiyasamy, msfs, is a member of the Missionaries of St. Francis de Sales (MSFS), a religious order known as the Fransalians. He has been working as pastor in different parishes for more than seventeen years in India and in the United States. At present he is the pastor of St. Mary parish in Flint in the Diocese of Lansing, Michigan. The author holds a Master of Arts in Tamil language from Annamalai University, Tamil Nadu, India, as well as a Doctor of Ministry in Biblical spirituality from Barry University in Florida. He is committed to serve God's people in the missions and loves to proclaim and promote the people-centered spirituality of Jesus and the optimistic spiritual wisdom of St. Francis de Sales.

About Leonine Publishers

Leonine Publishers LLC makes fine Catholic literature available to Catholics throughout the English-speaking world. Leonine Publishers offers an innovative "hybrid" approach to book publication that helps authors as well as readers. Please visit our web site at www.leoninepublishers.com to learn more about us. Browse our online bookstore to find more solid Catholic titles to uplift, challenge, and inspire.

Our patron and namesake is Pope Leo XIII, a prudent, yet uncompromising pope during the stormy years at the close of the 19th century. Please join us as we ask his intercession for our family of readers and authors.

Do you have a book inside you? Visit our web site today. Leonine Publishers accepts manuscripts from Catholic authors like you. If your book is selected for publication, you will have an active part in the production process. This book is an example of our growing selection of literature for the busy Catholic reader of the 21st century.

www.leoninepublishers.com